Wounded by Words

Wounded by Words

Healing the Invisible Scars
of Emotional Abuse

Susan Titus Osborn, MA
Karen L. Kosman
Jeenie Gordon, MS, MA, MFT

NEW HOPE
PUBLISHERS
Birmingham, Alabama

New Hope® Publishers
P. O. Box 12065
Birmingham, AL 35202-2065
www.newhopepublishers.com

New Hope Publishers is a division of WMU®.

Library of Congress Cataloging-in-Publication Data

Osborn, Susan Titus, 1944-
  Wounded by words : healing the invisible scars of emotional abuse /
Susan Titus Osborn, Jeenie Gordon, Karen L. Kosman.
    p. cm.
  ISBN 978-1-59669-049-3 (sc)
  1. Psychological abuse. I. Gordon, Jeenie. II. Kosman, Karen L.,
1942- III. Title.
RC569.5.P75O83 2008
616.85'82--dc22
                            2007017164

ISBN-10: 1-59669-049-6
ISBN-13: 978-1-59669-049-3

N074132 • 0208 • 4M1

Dedication

*This book is dedicated to all women
who have ever been "wounded by words."
May they find encouragement
and God's peace in these pages.*

Table of Contents

Caustic words and demeaning statements can be as dangerous to our well-being as any weapon. People often use words that dominate and control when they feel insecure themselves. Unfortunately these words are often directed at close family members, and the outcome is much pain and suffering. The tension resulting from these heated words often leads to the telling of lies by both parties.

Verbal abusers isolate, disorient, and indoctrinate their victims. Whether they are children or adults, the abused are usually family members. Depression, behavioral problems, and physical illnesses are a direct outcome of the emotional abuse. Often these results are not easily seen.

Standing in front of a mirror in a fun house is entertaining. We laugh at the distorted reflection looking back at us and then walk away from the experience. But the reflection in our minds that is created by emotional abuse is not dealt with so easily. Emotional abuse is a learned behavior for both abuser and victim. It undermines the foundation of the family. The victim of verbal abuse lacks confidence. She believes that others have a low opinion of her. The pattern of abuse creates feelings of rejection and worthlessness.

Chapter 4: *Sticks and Stones*

The old adage "Sticks and stones may break your bones, but names will never hurt you" is not true. Unkind words leave lasting scars, affecting how we deal with every aspect of our lives. An abused child, growing up in a dysfunctional home, will be the target of schoolyard bullies. Poor social skills aggravate this situation even more. A woman in a verbally abusive marriage may tend to withdraw, avoid social events, and become a recluse at work and even at church.

Chapter 5: *Telltale Signs*

Verbal abuse can affect our faith and cause us to move away from God. This often leads to poor choices and negative attitudes. Because victims often cover up what is going on in the home, they struggle with self-respect and show a lack of integrity. Because there are no visible wounds, the person is hesitant to ask for help from friends, family, or law enforcement.

Chapter 6: *Fork in the Road*

The victim continues to struggle on a daily basis. Old tapes continue to play in her mind, setting up a cycle of failure in relationships. Denial plays a major role, and the perception of self becomes distorted. Also, people have different perceptions of the same situation, and in order to communicate well, they have to come to an understanding of each other's views. These issues need to be faced before the person begins to heal. Then the victim can be set free.

Often we aren't able to communicate our true feelings to others. We have difficulty expressing the turmoil inside of us. Yet we look physically worn out, so those around us know something is wrong. Our appearance, posture, and tone of voice reveal our innermost thoughts. Our lack of confidence and low self-esteem become visible to others.

For years we have been subjected to emotional abuse. As a result, in our relationships with others, we tend to overreact, lose our cool, and act out the role of the abuser. In order to break this vicious cycle, we need to become aware this is happening. We aren't capable of changing on our own. We need to seek God's help and the help of others. We also need to pinpoint the triggers that set off these actions and to see them for what they are.

We need to lay down a new foundation with the Cornerstone being Jesus Christ. Through studying His Word, praying, and counseling, our distorted image of ourselves begins to change. We begin to erase the old, destructive tapes in our mind. Gradually our hope and faith are renewed. We come to the realization that we do not deserve to be put down with demeaning, caustic words.

Often during this healing process we are still living with our abuser. We need to learn to stand up for ourselves against this type of violence. Sometimes it may be possible to walk away from the situation to cool off and gain a better perspective. Counseling—where both parties are involved if possible or alone if not—is another alternative. In the workplace, verbal abuse should be reported. Learning what to do in different situations is a vital part of this process.

No one deserves to be emotionally abused. Find ways to refresh and relax away from the abuse. Learn to treat yourself with respect and to love yourself. Allow yourself to make new friends and to try new things. In time your confidence will build, opening up new opportunities for growth.

God knew us before He formed us in our mother's womb. Though we can only attempt to plan for our children's futures, God has planned the best for our lives. However, He has given us free will, so we can alter His plans by making poor choices. Ultimately, God has promised to never leave us or forsake us. In times of adversity He is shaping and molding us, and good will result. His everlasting arms are wrapped tightly around us. We are His children.

Introduction

L ouise rushed home from work to fix dinner for her four kids. Afterwards with the help of her oldest daughter, she put the three younger children to bed before her husband came home. Then she hurried back into the kitchen to prepare a special dinner for Edward. She grilled the filet mignon medium-rare, just the way he liked it. She fixed baked potatoes, green beans, and a Caesar salad. She thought, *If I can make everything perfect, maybe he won't yell at me, and we can have a peaceful evening.*

Interrupting Louise's thoughts, Edward barged through the front door. Glancing at his wife, he exclaimed, "I'm starved. Let's eat."

"It's all ready," Louise replied nervously. She watched him sit down at the table. Slowly she slid into her own seat.

Edward took one bite of his filet and made a face. Throwing his fork down, he shouted, "This meat is tough. I'd think after all these years you'd know how to fix my meat. What's wrong with you?"

Edward picked up his steak and flung it on the floor. Within seconds, Princess, the German shepherd, grabbed the meat and ran out the door. Then Edward stood up, shoved his chair away from the table, and walked out of the room.

Louise burst into tears. *Nothing I ever do satisfies him. What have I done wrong now? I try so hard to please him.*

What Louise didn't realize was that the fault didn't lie with her. No matter what she would have done, Edward would have found something to criticize her for. Edward was filled with pent-up anger that he tried to hide with alcohol, but it always resulted in abusing his family.

Since Louise was raising four small children, she felt trapped. She worked side-by-side with her husband in a successful business they owned. What would become of her if she left him? In time, this abusive action had a devastating affect not only on Louise but on her four children as they grew up and attempted to lead normal lives.

As a child, Edward, like most abusers, had been the victim in an emotionally abusive situation. Being victimized distorts a person's image of who he or she is. The unresolved anger inside creates a need to retaliate, and thus the victim becomes the abuser.

Louise's story is replayed over and over by thousands of women across the United States. This form of violence isolates, disorients, and indoctrinates the victim. If she doesn't share her situation with another, no one outside her immediate family becomes aware of what is going on.

Unlike physical abuse that leaves bruises and other visible wounds, the results of angry, thoughtless words are invisible, but nevertheless, the scars are there. These scars remain in hearts and minds, causing low self-esteem and lack of confidence.

The victim of this kind of abuse struggles with the question, "What is wrong with me?" She loses her identity, and when she tries to confront her abuser to get to the source of the problem, he denies that anything is wrong. He continually blames her for the state of affairs until she reaches a point where she believes him.

Accurate statistics are hard to find on verbal abuse, because many women aren't aware they are being abused. Others are ashamed and don't tell anyone what is happening in their lives. Yet surveys do show that verbal abuse exists in marriages and other family relationships, the workplace, nursing homes, college campuses, and many other situations. One out of four women admits to being verbally abused. In one study, 77 percent of women reported emotional abuse in combination with physical abuse. In this same study,

Wounded by Words

43 percent experienced emotional abuse as children or teenagers and 39 percent reported verbal abuse in a relationship within the last five years.

In Scripture, the stories of Leah, Joseph, Hannah, Job, Abigail, King David, Mary Magdalene, and Mary and Martha demonstrate examples of verbal abuse. How they overcame this invisible destroyer is encouraging to us all. These stories demonstrate how God dealt with emotional abuse in biblical times, and how He expects us to deal with this issue today, as well.

Growing up in an alcoholic home, Karen Kosman learned firsthand the pain of verbal abuse. Susan Osborn also was verbally abused by her mother. Later both women married men who continued the cycle of emotional abuse in their lives. Once again verbal abuse became part of the daily routine. Gradually through Scripture, counseling, and God's love, healing began in their lives. Today, both women are remarried to supportive, Christian husbands, and the cycle of abuse has been broken.

Lying in bed as a tiny girl, Jeenie Gordon listened to her father yelling—physically abusing her mother and breaking furniture. Jeenie's fragile heart was struck with terror. Her father had little respect for women, and years later, he verbally abused Jeenie and her sister. In turn, Jeenie married a man who carried on the verbal abuse. In her 25 years as a marriage and family therapist Jeenie has dealt with numerous patients who have also been emotionally abused.

These three women share their stories as well as the personal stories of many other individuals who, at various times in their lives, suffered demeaning, caustic words. Many of the names have been changed to protect these victims. The issues these people have learned to deal with will provide hope and wholeness for those who are in the process of finding answers.

Each chapter of this book offers hope and healing through Christ from these unseen and often overlooked hurts.

Wounded by Words

Connie L. Peters

Wounded by words—
No gaping hole
No blood
No bruise—
Only a deep unseen slash that pierces the soul.

It is more painful than any physical laceration.
It severs,
Paralyzes,
Aborts progress, productivity, and joy,
And sabotages a fulfilled life.

Lord, heal me from this wound.
Help me speak blessing and hope in return.
God, turn this around for my good,
And for the good of the person who wounded me.
Lord, all things are possible with you.

Let your Words have preeminence,
For your Words are truth—
A cleansing wash,
A healing balm.

You speak life and healing,
Hope and truth,
Joy and peace.
Let me be
Healed by Words.

CHAPTER I

Lethal Weapons

*Fathers, do not embitter your children,
or they will become discouraged.*
—Colossians 3:21

No one has escaped being wounded by words—whether young, elderly, quick, slow, skinny, or fat. All cultures, all races are affected. Words are powerful and make impressions on our hearts, minds, and souls. They can be used to tear down and destroy our self-esteem, forming a destructive foundation for our entire lives.

Verbal, physical, and sexual abuse are categorized as emotional abuse. When verbal abuse stands alone, it is difficult to detect because there are seldom physical scars. However, the result of being verbally abused eventually rears its ugly head and manifests itself in all aspects of a victim's life. Accurate statistics are difficult to obtain because denial, fear of more rejection, and low self-esteem keep a victim from reporting mistreatment. Verbal abuse toward children is seldom reported to Child Protective Services. Personal awareness and understanding of the issue are key to resolving the problem.

THE FOLLOWING STORY shows how a dad's angry words and thoughtless actions left a little girl feeling insecure and frightened.

"What a Stupid Thing to Do!"

Karen Kosman

Recently while I was grocery shopping, a woman with a cute little boy in tow walked past me. Smeared chocolate made a ring around his mischievous smile. His curly, brown hair and big, dark oval eyes instantly drew me to him. I waved, and he waved back with his free hand.

As I continued walking down the aisle, I lost sight of them. But moments later they rushed past me with the mom holding tightly to the toddler's arm.

"You're a bad boy! You can't come shopping with me anymore. You'll have to stay with a babysitter. I don't want you with me until you learn to keep your hands off things," she yelled at him. Tears streamed down his cheeks, and a look of bewilderment covered his face.

Stop! My mind screamed, *Don't you know the damage your angry words are causing?* I wanted to run after her, but I didn't. Instead I sighed and thought back to my own childhood and the angry words that surrounded me on a daily basis. Instantly, I was eight years old again—

One evening Dad's car pulled into our driveway. When he entered the house he asked me the question that I dreaded. "Karen, how'd you like to earn ten dollars babysitting your brother and sister while Mom and I go out?"

I felt afraid to tell Dad no, because I feared his anger and name-calling. I wiped my tears away as I watched him walk down the hall to the bathroom. I whispered to Mom, "Why go with him?"

"Karen, he doesn't drink as much when I'm with him."

I sighed, realizing nothing I could say would stop them from leaving.

After they were gone, every sound in the house became magnified. The dim yellow lightbulb flickered in the hallway and the wind howled outside. Then a branch from a shrub scraped against the dining room window.

Wounded by Words

What would I do if anything happened to one of the babies? I ran down the hallway and into their bedroom to check on them. Seven-month-old Diane slept peacefully, but Richard at 20 months had been sick. His raspy breathing frightened me. To be in charge at eight years old overwhelmed me. "Daddy, I don't want money, I want you and Mommy to stay home!" I sobbed.

In desperation, I ran to Mrs. Chambers, a neighbor who lived three houses down the street. The cold wind chilled me to the bone as I stood on her porch shivering. The door opened.

"Mom and Dad had to go out," I said tearfully.

"I'll come with you, Karen." Taking my hand, she walked me home and washed my face. Then we settled on the sofa with one of my favorite books.

When Mom and Dad came home, they found us reading. Mom thanked Mrs. Chambers, but Dad remained silent until she left.

"Karen," he shouted, "what a stupid thing to do! If she calls the police, do you know what can happen? Do you want the police to come and take Richard, Diane, and you away? You acted like a crybaby and caused a lot of trouble."

I ran to my room and fell on top of my bed sobbing. Then I remembered what Laura, our daytime babysitter, had told me about praying: "You can ask God for help anytime."

As I thought about the Bible stories Laura read to us, I whispered, "Dear God, I didn't mean to be bad. Please don't let the police take us away. I promise next time Daddy and Mommy go out I won't be stupid."

A comforting peace seemed to surround me after I prayed, and I didn't feel alone anymore. I closed my eyes and went to sleep.

After that experience Dad didn't ask Mom to go out with him anymore at night. Instead he stayed at his shop and drank. But I really don't think Mom would have gone with him anyway—the episode frightened her.

Before that night, I thought of God as a powerful, mysterious figure who remained out of reach. But that night, as I prayed and felt comforted, He became real to me.

●●●

Children have extremely tender hearts and are easily wounded by just a look or a word. In their innocence, they look up to adults, particularly parents, as a place of safety and security. Unable to operate at an adult level, they must trust—implicitly.

A father who could think no further than his next drink put a young girl in a dangerous position—one she was incapable of handling. Then he blamed and threatened her with the police taking away her and her siblings. As any child would, she took the blame entirely.

In essence, her dad told his precious daughter the incident was her fault and she could not be trusted. He implied she was nothing but a piece of junk. His actions and words sank deep within her troubled heart, bringing heartache, disillusionment, confusion, and terror.

Wisely she ran to her heavenly Father—the One who understood and cared. In His warm, loving arms, He caressed and comforted her aching heart.

> *The tongue of the wise commends knowledge,*
> *but the mouth of the fool gushes folly.*
> —Proverbs 15:2

I've Been Told
Charles R. Brown

You'll never amount to anything.
What a waste!
You know better than that.
Your dog has more sense than you do.
That's what I've been told.
What's the point?

You're always forgetting.
Can't you do anything right?
I wish you were dead!
That's what I've been told.

That was stupid.
I don't have time for your silliness.
What kind of answer is that?
Would you just go away?
That's what I've been told.

You idiot! Get out of the street!
Your brother never did that.
Don't embarrass us.
Why don't you think for a change?
That's what I've been told.

ALICIA'S STORY IS an example of how a mother's ill-placed accusations brought loneliness and confusion to her daughter.

It's Your Fault

Alicia Goodwin

"Alicia, get out!" Mom screamed. I knew I'd better move quickly. As soon as I ran outside, the door slammed behind me. I held my breath until I heard the click—the familiar sound of the door being locked behind me. Whenever Mom got angry, she always locked me outside.

I hadn't meant to knock my glass of milk over. I had watched, frozen in horror as the river of milk spread quickly across the table and fell to the floor. At an early age I'd learned that accidents were not allowed in our home.

I slowly walked to my swing set, sat down, and started swinging back and forth. The backyard had become my sanctuary. I breathed in the hot Louisiana humidity. I hoped the breeze would cool me. I looked up to heaven and said, "God, I know You're up there. I can see You." Talking with God helped me not to feel alone. "I want us to be happy. I want my mom to love me. Why doesn't she love me? God, am I really a bad girl?"

The following year, my parents divorced. I was in first grade. "It's all your fault your father left," Mom yelled at me. Her words tore at me day after day until I believed them.

The Christmas after they divorced Dad sent a skateboard and a Godzilla doll. I loved my presents, but Mom sent them back. I guess he gave up after that. When I heard that Dad had remarried, I cried and cried because it seemed to confirm that he had forgotten all about me.

"Alicia, your father never wanted you. Why else do you think he married a woman with three boys?"

I learned not to cry openly at Mom's words, but inside a voice chanted, *You are no good. No one will love you. Go away, little girl.*

In an uncanny way, Mom seemed to read my mind when she said, "You'll never amount to anything." Through the years Mom's words followed me everywhere I went and affected all aspects of my life.

Sometimes I wondered, *God, are You still there?*

My self-esteem reached an all-time low by the time I was an adolescent, and I began to look for approval in all the wrong places.

● ● ●

For a childish mishap, a mother threw her child out the door with a slam of finality. To be a disappointment to a parent is heartwrenching—especially when the incident is an accident. A child has no feasible way to make the situation right.

The broken heart of a little girl, rejected by both mother

and father, exudes through this story. She had no one to care for her, to love her, or to turn to.

Divorced parents often play the malicious role of condemning their former partners. This causes their children to truly believe they are unloved and unwanted.

It is not uncommon for parents to use their children as pawns to get back at their former spouses. Many of them go to great lengths—lying, throwing away cards and gifts, not telling the child the parent called, or skirting them off when it's time to be picked up for their every-other-weekend visit.

The angered parent often makes it so difficult on his or her former spouse (screaming telephone calls, swearing, lying, defying court orders) that the noncustodial parent gives up.

"I think my child will be better off without me and the hassles it causes for all of us" is a statement Jeenie has heard hundreds of times in therapy sessions. She encourages a parent to continue—no matter what. Giving up will have lifelong damaging emotional effects on the children.

THE FOLLOWING STORY portrays a nine-year-old boy who gave up sports because of the caustic words of his coach.

Just a Game
Angie Garrett

Tommy stepped up to the plate and took a few practice swings. At nine years of age, he struck a traditional batter's pose and waited for the pitch. It was midseason during his first year of baseball in the big game against a longtime rival. His team, one run down with two outs, was batting in the bottom of the ninth inning. Although he hadn't played the sport as long as some of the other boys, he gave it his all as he swung at the first pitch.

"Strike!"

Tommy shook off the umpire's call and again took a few

practice swings. The second pitch was low and hard. Tommy swung with all his might.

"Strike two!"

This time Tommy had to concentrate even harder as he waited for the pitch. His teammates on the bench grew louder as they anticipated his next move. The boy warming up to bat stopped in midswing to watch. Then came the ball.

"Strike three! You're out!"

Tommy hung his head and headed for the dugout, knowing that the game was over and his team had lost by only one run. He had dared to hope that he might tie the game with a base hit or maybe even a home run, but it hadn't happened. He looked up hopefully at the coach, thinking the man would at least appreciate his effort. It's just my first year, he thought. *I've only played half a season. What can he expect?*

Instead, the coach looked at him with a scowl. "We lost the game because of you, Tommy. You missed the ball. We could have won if you hadn't been at bat."

Tommy's love of baseball died that afternoon. He took the coach's words to heart and began to believe that he really did lose the game for his team. In spite of being reminded by his parents that baseball games have 27 outs per team and that other boys had also struck out during that particular game, Tommy began to dread going up to bat. He lost his confidence and dashed his dream of ever hitting a home run. He stopped trying.

Tommy never again played with the same spirit that he had before that day. While he managed to make it through the rest of that season, it was the last time he ever played a team sport. He didn't so much as participate in playground pickup games of kickball or neighborhood games of flag football and kick-the-can. In fact, he didn't do anything at all that was athletic unless forced to do so in PE class. His gym teachers could only coerce him into giving a halfhearted effort. Even in high school, when all of his friends were trying out for various school teams, Tommy hung back and showed little interest.

Today Tommy is both a father and a grandfather. He still shows no interest in sports. It comes as no surprise that his son and grandson don't either. Tommy had done nothing to encourage them to run and play as children are prone to do. They all sit and watch TV, exerting very little effort and burning little energy. It has become a family way of life—all because a coach made a game more than just a game.

● ● ●

"Tommy was so discouraged by an unkind, unthinking coach that it became a generational disease," says Jeenie. "He adopted the motto Give up, don't try. Who knows what Tommy and his son or grandson could have achieved had someone been in their corner to say it's OK. I believe in you. Let's practice every day in the backyard, or let's find another sport you will enjoy."

Susan's son, Richard, had a similar experience when he was in third grade. His baseball coach belittled him the entire season, and the other players teased him every time he missed a pitch. Richard never played Little League baseball again, but he turned his interest to swimming, and in high school he became an excellent backstroker. Today as a father of two little girls, he still swims for exercise. But he doesn't attend major-league baseball games nor follow either of the two local professional teams. The very mention of the phrase "Little League" still makes him feel uncomfortable.

Coaches don't realize the lasting effect their words can have on young minds. Children should play sports for fun and exercise, learning to work as a team along the way. Coaches need to encourage and teach them, instead of letting their own inflated egos get in the way. The old adage still holds: "It isn't whether you win or lose; it's how you play the game."

IN THE FOLLOWING STORY, God used a neighbor to help a mother overcome verbal and physical abuse of her two-year-old daughter.

Can't You Do Anything Right?

Kathy Collard Miller

Darcy's training pants were wet again. Again!

Marching over to my two-year-old daughter, I directed her into the bathroom. I felt frustrated as I struggled to pull down the soaking pants.

"Darcy, why can't you learn to use your potty chair?" I continued to berate her. "You just can't do anything right. I've told you countless times to use the potty chair, and you just have to disobey me, don't you?"

All the frustrations of the day spent taking care of this seemingly rebellious two-year-old and our newborn son closed in on me. I began spanking Darcy with my hand. My tension and tiredness found another outlet. Spanking changed to hitting.

Darcy's uncontrollable screaming brought me back to reason. Seeing the red blister on her bottom, I dropped to my knees.

"How can I act this way?" I sobbed. "I love Jesus. I don't really want to hurt my child. Oh God, please help me."

The rest of that day I held my anger in check. The next day started out pleasantly. I watched my happy daughter. *How could I ever be angry with you or want to hurt you?* I thought. But as the day progressed and pressures closed in on me, I became impatient. I looked forward to a few moments of peace while Darcy and two-month-old Mark took their naps.

Telling Darcy to play quietly in her room, I rocked Mark to sleep. Just as I laid him carefully into his crib, Darcy burst into the room shouting, "Mommy, I want to color."

Mark woke up crying. I grabbed Darcy by the shoulders, shook her, and screamed, "Shut up! Shut up! I want him to go to sleep!"

Both Darcy and Mark cried as I shoved Darcy aside, rushed out of the bedroom, and walked through the house, banging walls and slamming doors. Only after I kicked a kitchen cupboard and broke it did my anger subside.

As the weeks turned into months, my anger habit worsened. And my words constantly blamed Darcy for all of my problems and how I treated her.

I had been a Christian for ten years, and I felt ashamed. "Oh, God," I prayed over and over again, "please take away my anger." Yet no matter how much I prayed, I could not control my anger when Darcy didn't perform according to my desires. I turned into a screaming mother, and I began to wonder if I might kill Darcy in one of my next rages. In time, I had to be honest with myself—I was abusing her. "Oh God, no, I'm a child abuser! Help me!"

Inside I screamed for help, but I couldn't tell my husband. *After all, he's a policeman. He arrests people for the very things I'm doing.* I certainly couldn't tell my friends either. What would they think of me? I led a Bible study. They looked up to me as a strong Christian woman.

One day I realized Larry had left his off-duty service revolver in the bureau drawer. Suicidal thoughts plagued me. If I kill myself, I won't hurt Darcy anymore. But then the thought sprang into my mind. *But if people hear a Christian like me committed suicide, what will they think of Jesus?* I couldn't bear the thought that Jesus's name would be maligned.

God, don't You care? I need instant deliverance from my anger. I'm in a pit of despair and depression.

One day, I shared briefly with a neighbor friend about my anger. She didn't condemn me. She even indicated she felt angry toward her children, too. "Oh, Lord, maybe there's hope for me after all," I cried out when I left her house that day.

From that point on, God seemed to break through my despair, and little by little He revealed the underlying causes and the solutions for my anger. And there were many.

I learned how to identify my anger before it became destructive. I forced myself to believe God wanted to forgive me—over and over again. After reading books about disciplining children effectively, I became more consistent in responding calmly to Darcy's disobedience. As a result, she became better behaved.

I also copied verses onto cards, placing them in various locations throughout the house. As I took Darcy into the bathroom, I was reminded, *"Hatred stirs up dissension, but love covers over all wrongs"* (Proverbs 10:12). This verse and others helped break my cycle of anger. Through a difficult process of growth over a year, God's Holy Spirit empowered me to be the loving, patient mother to Darcy that I wanted to be.

● ● ●

Kathy gained deep insight to help her overcome her abusive attitude through 2 Corinthians 10:5: *"We demolish arguments and every pretension that sets itself up against the knowledge of God, and we take captive every thought to make it obedient to Christ."*

God helped Kathy through Scripture and prayer to seek help, forgive herself, trust Him, and to find joy. Today Kathy has a close relationship with her beautiful 30-year-old daughter, who has completely forgiven her.

Unfortunately, many mothers don't realize what effect their caustic words and actions have on their children—actions often remembered for a lifetime. The actions of Susan's mother caused Susan, at a very young age, to lose the ability to trust her mother.

ONCE THAT BOND was broken, it became difficult to mend.

The Piggy Bank
Susan Titus Osborn

One afternoon I sat on my bed and shook all the money out of my piggy bank. As an eight-year-old, I'd learned to be frugal.

My mother came into the room and looked at the mound of coins on my bed. She looked startled. "What's this?" she asked with a frown.

I smiled and said, "I'm counting all the money in my piggy bank." She sat down on the bed and stared at the mound of coins. "I'll help you count it."

We discovered that I had collected over $100 in dimes, quarters, and silver dollars.

"I'll take care of these for you," she said as she walked out the door, carrying my money in a plastic sack.

Where is she going with my money? Will I ever see it again? I'd worked hard to save my money. My daddy gave me an allowance, which I rarely spent. I almost always put the coins in my piggy bank. I could do extra chores for more money, and I put the coins from those in my bank, too.

I spent almost every weekend with my grandparents. When my grandfather came home after his golf game, he took off his jacket and said, "Susan, you can have any change you find in my coat pockets. He watched me with a twinkle in his eye as I eagerly searched through all his pockets. I always found money tucked away in one pocket or another. My grandfather made sure I didn't come up empty-handed. Occasionally, I'd find a shiny silver dollar. I took all those coins and silver dollars and added them to my piggy bank.

But now my pink piggy bank lay empty on its side in the middle of my bed, and I had an uneasy feeling in the pit of my stomach.

I forgot the incident for a while. When I thought of it again, I realized that my mother hadn't opened a checking or savings account for me like so many of my friends had. Nor had she bought me something special with my money. As a matter of fact, she never mentioned my money again. And I never said a word about it either, but I realized, *I will never see that money again. Mother can't be trusted.*

I never again kept my money in my pink piggy bank. Piggy sat empty on my dresser, while my money, which I once again began to collect, lay in the bottom of my toy box, safely tucked away in old sock puppets.

● ● ●

With God's help, Susan has forgiven her mother for taking her money and for many other incidents that happened so long ago, causing her emotional abuse. Yet, once in a while, the memory of an incident pops to the surface, and Susan once again prays for the ability to forgive.

The old adage "Forgive and forget" is untrue. Forgiveness means we give up our right to retaliate and not seek revenge. Yet, residual feelings remain—anger, hurt, and similar emotions. However, these feelings will be fleeting momentary segments. We can handle the moments, because they no longer have a stranglehold on our lives.

Children are wide-eyed, innocent, and trusting. They are also eager to forgive. It takes a lot for a child to distrust a parent. When it happens, as it did to Susan, she learned a lifelong lesson. As is normal, she did not bring up the subject to her mother, for a child hasn't much of a leg to stand on when it comes to adults. Children can be stripped of their paltry rights quickly and easily by an overpowering grownup. Susan learned it was in her best interest to keep quiet.

Susan chose a different approach with her own children. When they were young, she set up savings accounts for them and told them how money can grow if you let the bank use it for a while. But she never told them about her pink piggy bank or any other incident that would tarnish the boys' opinion of their grandmother.

Throughout the Bible, God shows many examples of physical, verbal, sexual, and emotional abuse as well as guidelines for loving one another and communicating with respect and kindness. Jesus used parables to teach His disciples as well as His other followers how to follow these guidelines.

In Matthew 18:1, the disciples asked Jesus, "Who is the greatest in the kingdom of heaven?"

Jesus answered them by having a little child come and stand among them. Then Jesus said: *"I tell you the truth, unless you change and become like little children, you will never enter the kingdom of heaven. Therefore, whoever humbles himself like this child is the greatest in the kingdom of heaven"* (vv. 3–4).

Because children are trusting by nature, trusting their heavenly Father comes naturally. Adults who influence young children are held accountable to God for how they affect these little ones' ability to trust.

Jesus went on to issue a warning:

> *And whoever welcomes a little child like this in my name welcomes me. But if anyone causes one of these little ones who believe in me to sin, it would be better for him to have a large millstone hung around his neck and to be drowned in the depths of the sea* (Matthew 18:5–6).

Jesus obviously cares very much for children, and He is concerned about what happens to them—physically, verbally, sexually, and emotionally.

Reflections

Describe an incident in your life during which you experienced words used as lethal weapons.

*Lord, help me to heal from the wounds
that lethal words have caused.*

CHAPTER 2

Invisible Scars

Guard my life and rescue me;
let me not be put to shame,
for I take refuge in you.
—Psalm 25:20

Verbal abusers isolate, disorient, and indoctrinate their victims. Whether they are children or adults, the abused are usually family members. Depression, behavioral problems, and physical illnesses are often direct outcomes of emotional abuse—often resulting in invisible scars.

Merriam Webster's Collegiate Dictionary, 11th Edition, defines the word *scar* as the outcome of a troubled experience, as well as the beginning of a healing process. For the most part, we all hope that our pain, wounds, and scars will result in healing.

THE FOLLOWING STORY shows the invisible scars left on Susan and her two sons by their father.

The Accident
Susan Titus Osborn

"Richard, what happened?" I gasped as the front door opened and my oldest son walked in. His head was bleeding, and he had a petrified look on his face.

His brother Mike followed and said, "If you think he looks bad, wait until you see the car!"

"I don't care about the car. I care about you two. What happened?" I asked again.

"We dropped off a couple of the guys after water polo practice. Dave was hanging out the window, so I reached over and pulled him back in," said Richard.

"And the car rolled forward and hit a tree," added Mike. "Richard had unfastened his seat belt, so when the car stopped, he hit the windshield. I think he did more damage to the car than the tree did."

I saw that the cut on Richard's forehead was minor, so I cleaned it up and put a bandage on it. "Do you hurt anywhere? Do you feel dizzy?"

"My neck hurts," Richard said, rubbing the back of his neck."

"We'd better get that checked out at the emergency room," I said. I opened the front door and looked at the car. The front window was shattered. "Oh no! We probably shouldn't drive that car. I'll call Dad at work. It's 7:00 P.M. Surely he can come home and take us to the hospital."

I dialed my husband's office number. When he answered I said, "Richard's been in a car accident. His head broke the windshield, and his neck is injured." My voice sounded on the edge of hysteria. "He drove home after the accident, but I'm afraid to drive him to the hospital with the windshield broken. Can you please come home right away and take us?"

"No, I'm in a business meeting," was his curt reply.

"We really need you to drive us to the hospital!" I pleaded.

"I said no! You deal with it!" he shouted. Then he hung up on me.

Acid churned in my stomach, but I said in a resigned voice, "Come on, Richard. I'll take you to the emergency room." Fighting back tears, I slowly drove the damaged station wagon to the hospital, which, thankfully, was nearby.

I sat in the stillness of the waiting room while Richard went through a thorough examination and had some x-rays taken. My husband's reaction and his lack of concern played over and over in my mind. *Why wouldn't he come home? This certainly registered as an emergency! Doesn't he care about his family anymore?*

I thought back over the past few years and realized that little by little, my husband had emotionally removed himself from the boys and me. He traveled half of the time, so he was also physically removed. He put money in the checking account and left town. I took it from there. I paid the bills, made all the decisions, and planned our activities—the boys' and mine.

Actually, in my husband's absence our home remained peaceful, but the minute he returned from a business trip, the tension mounted. His complaining always began over little things that didn't matter.

"Where's my newspaper? How can I find anything in this mess?"

"Your newspaper is on the kitchen table, probably under a school book."

"Susan, the boys' water polo balls and equipment don't belong by the front door. Nor do school books belong on the kitchen table. I'm sick and tired of this mess."

"The boys always do their homework on the kitchen table. And they need their water polo equipment by the front door, or they'll forget it," I replied with exasperation.

"My hotel room is always spotless when I return to it, but just look at this place!"

Of course two teenage boys hadn't spent the afternoon in his hotel room…Did he really prefer a clean room to his family?

Our lives were peaceful and fun when it was just the three of us. Soon after that conversation, Richard confided in me. "Mom, we can't stand to see Dad talk down to you. It's abusive, and you just stand there and take it. That's hard on us, too."

"I know," I replied weakly, giving him a hug, "but I really don't know how to stop him."

Richard just shrugged his shoulders in reply.

While I sat in the waiting room by myself, God used Richard's accident to open my eyes to our situation. Remembering what Richard had said to me weeks earlier, I thought of some of the snide comments my husband often made: "Are you fixing that again for dinner?" "Can't you anticipate what I want?" "What's wrong with you?" Shivering, I rubbed my arms at the thought. *Did I really want to retire and spend the rest of my life with this man who showed me no love or concern?*

As I continued to sit and ponder, I realized that my husband's demeaning statements had left invisible scars on our hearts. I began to understand the overwhelming effect those scars might have on our lives. He never hit us, but the hurt he inflicted destroyed our self-confidence.

The following year the verbal abuse escalated and other circumstances became unbearable, causing my health to deteriorate. I developed ulcers, huge chunks of my hair fell out, and my left side went numb. My wise family doctor suggested that I file for a legal separation and referred me to a Christian psychologist.

I followed his advice and then called the boys in for a family conference. I said, "I went to a lawyer today, and I'm going to ask your dad to live elsewhere for a while."

Mike nodded his agreement, but Richard said, "Why didn't you do that 2 years ago, Mom? Look at all we've been through."

"Richard, I had 22 years invested in your dad, and I wanted to try and save our marriage. I had to make sure that he wasn't willing to work things out before I took this major step. Now I'm sure. I'm sorry for the pain that we've caused you both."

I gave my oldest son a hug, and then I turned and embraced Mike. We stood there for a long time in a three-way hug, and I knew everything would work out with God's help.

There is a well-known story about a frog that applies to Susan's circumstances. If you place a frog in boiling water, he will jump out. But if you submerge a frog in warm water, he feels comfortable. If the water is slowly heated to a higher temperature, he continues in a false contentment because he is not aware of the change. The result is boiled frog legs for dinner. Looking back, Susan says, "I can see that the verbal abuse started gradually and increased so slowly that I really wasn't aware of what was happening to me until I was scalded. And then, like the frog, it was too late."

It takes two people to make a marriage work, but only one to destroy it. Susan's first husband had forsaken the relationship, and he was not willing that it be restored. Obviously, Susan's husband was a controller. He manipulated his family by blaming them—nothing was ever good enough.

Generally, a controller is one who was abused (physically, sexually, emotionally) in childhood. Because children have such tender hearts, no child is able to stand up to an abusive parent. Therefore, they continue to take the abuse.

However, often children will vow, *When I grow up, I'll never let anyone abuse me again.* This decision, often made at a young age, is carried into their adult lives, and they try to control everyone and everything that comes into their path. But actually, the converse is true. The greater the need to control, the more out of control they actually become. Therefore, they choose to marry a person who will succumb—someone who will not make waves or rock the boat—someone who will suffer in silence so they can become the controller.

The family of a controller is typical of Susan's—members who continue to try to please never make it. They never can. The controlling continues to escalate. Relief is only felt when the family is physically removed from the controlling influence. If they stay in the situation, they feel trapped.

So often these family members are afraid to let go, to get out of the situation. They cling to a false hope that things will change. Yet, they don't have the ability to change another person—only God can. And that person must want to change in order for God to work in his life.

What Words Can Do
Connie L. Peters

Words are like colors to an artist,
they lift the spirit or
express the disappointments and
tragedies of life.

Words are like sounds to the musician,
creating songs to dance,
celebrate, mourn, or worship.

Words are like tools to a carpenter
to build up or to tear down.

Words are like medicine to a doctor,
given at the proper time and dosage they can heal,
but given improperly they can kill.

Words are like food to the hungry
and water to the thirsty,
or they can be like poison.

Words can build up or tear down.
Words can create or destroy.
Words can heal or hurt.
Words can nourish or starve.
Words can comfort or wound.

May the words of my mouth and the meditation of my heart be
pleasing in your sight, O LORD, my Rock and my Redeemer.
—Psalm 19:14

DR. MARY SIMMS had a client named Jim, a pastor who helped other people find answers to their problems. Yet he felt overwhelmed by his own emotional turmoil.

Trapped
Dr. Mary M. Simms

"I feel trapped," Pastor Jim said as he sat down for counseling in my office. He had taken care of others all of his life, and now he was the one seeking help. It took a lot of courage for him to come to me. Normally he was seated in the position where I now sat, and so many people looked to him for answers to their problems.

I could hear the anguish in his voice. It seemed as if he had been holding onto the pain for a long time.

"I have been in a difficult marriage for 28 years, and I don't know what to do." Jim sighed and then continued, "Now that my children are grown, I don't think there is any reason to stay in the marriage other than the fact that I am a Christian minister and I want to please God. But I don't know how long I can last with the emotional pain that I am going through."

I looked at Jim compassionately. "Let's work on your marital issues," I suggested, "since you are the one who is willing to try to solve your problems. We can't do anything about your wife's 'stuff' because she refuses to come with you, but we can look at your issues."

After some resistance, he agreed. In talking about his history, Jim revealed that he had built up resentment over many years toward his wife. In the weeks of counseling that followed, further discovery showed that much of his bitterness was buried inside him. Although he didn't express this outwardly to his wife, this wall Jim built around his heart kept him from achieving emotional intimacy with her.

"I can't talk to her," he said. "She always interrupts me and never lets me get a word in. Most of the time I just give in because it is not worth the conflict."

"Conflict is an inevitable part of marriage. It's not the actual disagreement, but how you work through it that matters," I said.

Jim stated that in both his married life as well as in his professional life he had a difficult time dealing with conflict. He found himself withdrawing from arguments and shutting down while resentment built up inside.

As I began to help Jim take the focus off his wife, I could look deeper to see where his wounds might be. I asked him, "How was conflict handled when you were growing up?"

He replied, "Conflict in my childhood home was never handled at all. There was no room for working things out or having disagreements. Mom yelled, demanding certain attitudes and behaviors from her children, and we gave her what she wanted. That was it. Period. There was no room to negotiate!"

"Tell me more about your parents," I suggested.

He responded, "Oh, Dad was in and out of my life, and he left the family when I was ten years old. Mom seemed to always be the strong one, but when Dad left, she became angry and controlling, especially toward me. Perhaps it was because I looked a lot like Dad."

Jim went on to say, "Many times Mom made me responsible for my two sisters and younger brother. One time, when I was only 13, my 8-year-old sister went to a neighbor's house instead of coming home from school. When Mom came home, she was frantic. 'Jim, you should know better. What is wrong with you? If something happens to your sister, I am going to hold you accountable!' After verbally abusing me, she beat me with a leather belt."

Looking at the ground, he continued, "Mom's wrath was difficult to reckon with. She seemed to always be angry, even when I tried to make things better for her."

In working with Jim, I realized that he was often angry at his mother while growing up, but he didn't have permission to express it. Jim learned how to develop a conforming personality, but inwardly he stuffed his feelings. As a result, he built up deep resentment. Yet, he vowed that he would be a boy who Mom could be proud of.

"Mom worked a lot, and because of her single parent status with four children, she often came home angry. She always projected her anger onto me. 'Why is the house not cleaned?' she asked. If the floor was not scrubbed the way that she wanted, she questioned, 'What is wrong with you? Are you stupid? Can't you do anything right?'"

She wounded him with words and then beat him physically if things were not done to her expectations.

"There was never any affirmation," Jim said. "I felt as though I always fell short."

"Is that the way you sometimes feel regarding your wife?" I asked.

"Yes," he replied. At that moment he realized that the wounds he had experienced during his childhood in his relationship with his mother made it difficult to see with clarity the issues with his wife.

When his wife expressed a need like wives often do, he interpreted it as if she was a demanding, controlling person and built resentment toward her. Helping him to connect to his real feelings and find his voice again was crucial. As Jim began to take ownership of his pain and surrender those powerless, angry little-boy feelings to God, his healing process began.

He started communicating better with his wife. He no longer retreated from his feelings and was willing to share his deep emotional needs. As he responded more positively in his marital relationship, his wife felt the need to look at her issues, and she joined him for counseling.

It is amazing how comfortable people become in a dysfunctional, unhealthy relationship! Eventually, the situation feels normal to them. So, what do they do? Usually they end up marrying into the same type of setting they grew up in because that is what they are used to. Seldom do they marry a healthy person, because that would be foreign to the lifestyle to which they have become accustomed.

Jim married a woman just like Mom. In growing up, he needed to obey his mother's demands—and did. However, the internal hurt was enormous. So in order for him to survive emotionally, he began to disconnect from her.

When Jim sensed the same issues in his marriage and felt the first stab of rejection, childhood memories flooded in. Old feelings surfaced. So, little by little, he backed off emotionally from his wife. It hurt too much to stay close. Eventually, the chasm was so great he did not believe it could ever be reconnected. Divorce was not an option for Jim, and he felt despondent.

Jim could have continued to suffer in silence, but he made a wise choice. He decided to seek professional help.

● ● ●

IN THE FOLLOWING STORY Robin Aoks thinks back in time to a visit from her father that she would never forget. As she puts it, "My dad's words were burned into my heart, mind, and soul—invisible scars never to be forgotten."

I Am Not a Mistake
Robin Aoks

Over the years, news of my dad came to me through family members. He'd dumped his second wife to take up with the woman who would soon become his third wife. Now after all these years he was flying to San Diego to take me out to dinner. As a fairly new Christian I prayed for the strength to face my dad—someone who'd been like a stranger to me.

My date with Dad took a pungent turn when he brought me back home. He parked in front of my apartment building. As I started to get out of his rental car, he grabbed my arm and pleaded, "Wait. I want to explain what happened."

I sat back, not really sure I wanted to hear what he had to say. "Robin, everyone makes mistakes in life. I'm no different, but I've tried hard to correct my mistakes," he mumbled. "The only reason I married your mother was because she was pregnant."

Although he continued on with his gentle tone, pleading for understanding, even acknowledging his actions and current situation, everything inside me had stopped. *I am the child produced from that pregnancy,* my mind screamed.

Dad continued, his words describing himself as the most noble of men. Carefully he listed his reasons for marrying and leaving his first two wives, ending with the statement that he would finally marry someone he "truly loved."

I sat silently during his soliloquy. I acknowledged with a grunt that I had heard him, but my thoughts were fixated on why he had married my mom. My dad had just called me a mistake, an unwanted child. Dad's words echoed in my head, *I married your mom so she would not be an unwed mother.* I had heard so much more than he intended.

"Good-bye, Dad," I whispered, holding back my tears. Then I quickly stepped out of the car. My heart hemorrhaged from a wound that seemed to threaten the core of my existence.

I slowly walked into my apartment, my arms across my chest, holding my sides tightly, trying to hold back the pain. I tiptoed to my room and carefully closed the door. I didn't want my roommates to know I'd come home. I didn't want to be disturbed. My world had been flipped upside down.

I started crying and couldn't stop. Sobbing, I grabbed my Bible and flipped it open. My vision blurred, and I had trouble reading the words, but I desperately needed God.

"Lord," I whispered, "am I a mistake? Am I not wanted? If that is true, what will I do? How can I continue to live?"

As I flipped through the pages, my eyes fell on a passage, and I started reading: *"Before I formed you in the womb I knew you, before you were born I set you apart"* (Jeremiah 1:4–5).

"Oh God, I'm not a mistake. You knew me before You formed me. You planned my birth." In that moment I realized my heavenly Father had an unconditional love for me and a plan for my life.

● ● ●

Robin wisely turned to God's Word for her self-worth, as well as attending a professional counseling group. Over the next two years, through research and group therapy, Robin came to realize that her dad was a narcissist.

The verbal abuse of a narcissist is hard to spot. Nina Brown, in her book, *Children of the Self-Absorbed: A Grown-up's Guide to Getting Over Narcissistic Parents*, describes a narcissist as follows:

> Parents with a destructive narcissistic pattern will have behaviors and attitudes that are designed to preserve a self-image of perfection, entitlement, and superiority. For the child's entire life the parent-child relationship was reversed, and the child, even after attaining adulthood, is expected to:
> * absorb parental projections
> * accept blame and criticism
> * automatically know what the parent wants or needs and give it to him or her
> * admire the parent and give unlimited attention
> * never offend the parent
> * understand that he or she is inferior to the parent and not react to demeaning comments
> * realize that the parent will always know what is best for the child

Adult children of parents who have a destructive narcissistic pattern will continue to feel the impact of their parent's behavior and attitudes and continue to suffer reactions that are as perplexing to them as they are distressing.

With destructive, narcissistic parents, the focus is always on themselves, while the child's wishes are totally ignored—neither seen nor acknowledged. That feeling of being inherently flawed grows with the years and continues into adulthood, with the following thought pattern: *If I'm flawed, then I'm unlovable. If I'm flawed to the point that even my own parents cannot love me, then there is no expectation of there ever being anyone who could even like, much less love, me. If I'm flawed, then nothing I do is worth contributing—for any work I attempt would also be flawed.*

Yet God can break this destructive cycle. He does not make junk. He loves us unconditionally, and He has a plan for each of our lives. He desires that each of us have our own voice, and He helps us to find it.

Sometimes verbal abuse comes from another member of the family rather than the parent. We find such a story, the account of a woman named Hannah, in the Old Testament book of 1 Samuel, the first chapter. Her story is one of infertility, trouble, depression, bitterness, and verbal abuse. Yet, it's also about faith and courage that helped her to overcome.

What would it be like to share your husband with a second wife—one who had borne him sons and daughters while you remained childless? Now add jealousy and verbal abuse from your rival—the other wife—and you have dysfunction and misery.

Perhaps you think that because this drama unfolded in a culture where women were considered subservient to men that Hannah's story does not relate to yours. Yet, it is the human reaction to verbal abuse we want to compare. What does God want us to learn from Hannah's story?

The people described in 1 Samuel 1 were flesh and blood, mind and spirit. They lived like you and me. Although Scripture does not give a complete dialogue between Elkanah's wives, Peninnah and Hannah, it does tell us in verse 6, *"Her rival kept provoking her in order to irritate her. This went on year after year."*

Imagine you are Hannah. Your eyes are swollen and red from crying, and your heart is breaking. It's difficult to sleep and eat when your arms ache to hold a child—your child. Where do you go to find the answer to a problem that seems unsolvable? The tears begin once again, and with your sobs your body trembles.

Elkanah heard the sound of weeping and pondered, *Peninnah and her jealousy have been at work again. I'll go to my wife Hannah and comfort her.*

You feel a gentle hand touch your shoulder, "Hannah, why are you weeping? Why don't you eat? Why are you downhearted? Don't I mean more to you than ten sons?"

Elkanah's last question indicates that he loved Hannah regardless of her barren womb.

Every year Elkanah would take his family from their hometown of Ramah, a city in the hill country of Ephraim, and travel to Shiloh. There in the temple they would worship and sacrifice to the Lord Almighty.

Year after year Peninnah verbally abused Hannah because of her infertility. Hannah felt disgraced. During one of their trips to Shiloh, Hannah turned to God in her anguish.

She prayed with great emotion, silently with her lips moving, as she poured out her heart to the Lord.

> *"O Lord Almighty. If you will only look upon your servant's misery and remember me, and forget not your servant but give her a son, then I will give him to the Lord for all the days of his life, and no razor will ever be used on his head."*
>
> —1 Samuel 1:11

The priest, who was named Eli, thought she was drunk, and he said to her, *"How long will you keep on getting drunk? Get rid of your wine"* (v. 14).

Hannah's reply was heartwrenching:

"Not so, my Lord, I am a woman who is deeply troubled. I have not been drinking wine or beer; I was pouring out my soul to the Lord. Do not take your servant for a wicked woman; I have been praying here out of my great anguish and grief."

—1 Samuel 1:14–16

Something in this woman's eyes told Eli that she spoke the truth, and he said, *"Go in peace, and may the God of Israel grant you what you have asked of him"* (v. 17).

Living with humiliation, Hannah turned to God, and through His sovereignty she found faith and hope. The Lord blessed Hannah with a son, and she named him Samuel. Hannah kept her vow to dedicate her son to God. From about the age of three, Samuel grew up in the temple under the guidance of Eli in the service of the Lord. Samuel became the most effective judge of Israel. God rewarded Hannah for her faithfulness, and she gave birth to three more sons and two daughters.

Lessons we learn from Hannah:
- She sought help by bringing her troubles to God.
- She prayed.
- She worshipped.
- She trusted God.

The *World Book Dictionary* (http://www.worldbook.com) defines invisible as: "not capable of being seen—too small to be perceived—so dark as to be hardly distinguishable from black." That's how invisible scars look and feel to the victim.

Rarely are invisible scars detected by others. They may see the outward behaviors, but the scars remain invisible. Without a moment's rest the pain, torture, and churning goes on for years within the depth of one's soul.

But there's hope! As we allow God to weave the tapestry of our lives, it will eventually become a thing of beauty. The ugly underside will no longer haunt us when we view the completed masterpiece. The gold threads will shimmer as they stand out against the black background.

Reflections

Describe an emotional pain that has left a scar on your self-esteem.

Lord, heal my invisible scars that careless, angry words have created.

CHAPTER 3

Distorted Images

Do everything without complaining or arguing,
so that you may become blameless and pure, children of God
without fault in a crooked and depraved generation,
in which you shine like stars in the universe
as you hold out the word of life.
—Philippians 2:14–16

Actions as well as words often communicate negative feelings. In a moment of rage, adults may not see children standing nearby listening, as their young minds record abusive words.

As an example imagine this scenario. A door slams so hard the pictures on the wall vibrate. Immediately, a little girl stops playing and retreats to her bedroom closet, taking her babydoll with her. Inside the confines of her closet, she turns on the light and sits on the floor. There she feels removed from the volatile situation about to erupt. There she feels safe. Why did this little girl respond in this manner?

In a dysfunctional family where verbal abuse is common, other warning signs may be an angry look, a clenched fist, or an alcoholic with a drink in his hand. These can be signals to the rest of the family that a verbal rampage is about to occur. These behaviors create learned responses from other family members that contribute to the distorted self-image of the abused.

IN THE FOLLOWING STORY we see a little girl's reaction to some of these telltale signs that interrupt a fun night out with family.

Fun House Images
Karen L. Kosman

A neon sign in brilliant red and blue colors flashed the words "Fun House," and just above it an animated woman rocked back and forth laughing. My brother, Richard, and sister, Diane, rushed past me to get in line with Dad. Mom lagged behind with me and my baby brother, Roy, and said, "Go ahead, Karen, have some fun. I'll wait right here."

Once we were inside the fun house, I chose a door and opened it. I found myself standing in a small room with mirrors plastered across the walls. Unlike the mirrors at home, these distorted my image. In one I looked round like a balloon; in another my image was stretched out like a rubber band.

Abruptly, Dad, Richard, and Diane entered the same room. Richard made a funny face and stuck out his tongue. Diane did a handstand, and then they both broke out in laughter at the crazy, cartoon-type images the mirrors reflected. Preoccupied with watching my younger siblings, I hadn't noticed Dad standing behind me.

Then a whiff of alcohol caught my attention. Dad's reflection in the mirror contorted his face, and his body stretched into wavy fingers. The truth of his internal image struck me to the core—ugly, awful, sick. This was not the image I held in my heart of Dad. Everything within me screamed: *No, no, this can't be my dad.*

Yet, I knew what would happen later, and I felt an overwhelming sadness—a feeling not uncommon to me when Dad combined family fun with his need to drink. In a matter of minutes I had gone from happiness to dread. I wanted to do something to stop the emotional upheaval that often followed a night out—the name-calling, the arguments, and the tears. Would tonight be any different?

"Can we leave now?" I asked. Then I turned and ran out of the room, making my way back through the maze of the fun house. Once outside I took a deep breath of fresh air.

My mind swirled. *It hasn't always been this way. I remember a time when Dad didn't yell, a time when he seemed more like a gentle giant to me. At bedtime he'd tuck me in and read nursery rhymes. We'd laugh together.*

After he read "Twinkle, Twinkle, Little Star" one night, he promised, "Princess, someday I'm going to paint stars on your bedroom ceiling, and they are going to sparkle."

Sometimes he'd take me on a date, just Dad and me. I felt special. The change in him had come gradually. Two incidents that sent a warning that something was terribly wrong occurred almost simultaneously.

The first was on a night when the front door slammed. Waking up, I tiptoed out of bed and searched for my mom, but she had left. Dad stood in the living room, his body swaying unsteadily. I felt afraid, so I snuck out to our screened patio. My body shivered from the cold. "Where did Mom go?" I whispered to myself as I curled up on an old sofa.

Then I heard Dad call, "Karen, where are you?" I didn't want to answer, but I knew I'd better. I made my way into the living room.

"What are you doing out of bed?" Dad shouted.

"Where's Mom?"

"Get to bed, and don't get up again."

He staggered toward me, and I turned and ran into my bedroom. At five I didn't understand what it all meant. I thought I must have done something terrible. *Dad doesn't love me anymore. He doesn't tuck me in bed anymore.* I cried myself to sleep, not sure what the morning would bring.

In the morning I found Mom in the kitchen cooking breakfast as if nothing had happened. She made no comment about the night before. After breakfast she said, "Time to get ready for school."

The second incident occurred a week or so later when my best friend's parents came over to talk with mine. Mom said, "Karen, go play in your room for a while."

I obeyed, but the closed bedroom door didn't keep their voices out. "We wanted you to know why Joan can't play here anymore," Mrs. Allen said.

"I don't understand. Why? Karen and Joan are good friends," Mom replied.

Their voices escalated. "You're a drunk!" my friend's dad announced to my dad and then slammed the front door.

My bedroom door opened, and Mom came in and sat down on my bed next to me. I burst into tears. I looked at her swollen pregnant stomach and her red tear-streaked face, and I stopped crying.

"What does *drunk* mean?" I asked.

"It means Dad drinks too much beer and wine."

"Why?" I asked.

"I don't know why, Karen, and I don't know what to do to make things better."

I reached over and patted Mom's hand.

From that moment on I told myself: *If I'm a good girl and help, maybe Dad will love me again. Maybe he'll paint stars on my ceiling. Maybe he won't drink wine and beer anymore.*

Often friends and family would say, "Karen is so grown up. You must be proud of her."

"Yes, I am proud of her," Mom would reply.

If they'd only understood that behind the mask of a grown-up Karen a little girl hid and cried silently. I learned when to sneak off to my room to avoid the angry words and insults shouted by Dad. There were no more special times with just Dad and me going for dinner or out to a movie, and he didn't call me his princess anymore.

I continued to act the mature girl, always good, always helpful, always obedient, and I waited for the stars on my ceiling—but they never appeared.

● ● ●

Wounded by Words

Karen believed in her tender child's heart if she tried harder and made herself good enough, that her dad wouldn't drink, and they could be a happy family. Imagine the huge burden these thoughts put on such young shoulders. Karen truly believed her actions, and hers alone, could change the scenario of a drunken father. This is a typical reaction for a child of an alcoholic.

The action of Karen's mom is typical of a wife living with an alcoholic husband. Even though her heart is undoubtedly aching for her children, she pretends everything is OK and carries on as if nothing has happened. Basically, everyone knows about Dad being a drunk, but the family acts like things are normal, and it is not a subject that is ever addressed with honesty.

Cover-up is par for the course. A wife often calls in "sick" at work for her husband, explaining he has a terrible case of the flu and has been vomiting. Actually he is throwing up the liquor he consumed. Or, moms ask the children to be quiet because "Dad isn't feeling well."

We read in Genesis 1 that God made the stars to give light to the earth, to govern the day and night, and to separate the darkness from the light. And ever since the beginning of creation, people have shown an interest in the beauty of the heavens above. Astronomers study the moon, stars, and surrounding planets, trying to understand the entire workings of the universe. Seagoing men have charted their courses by the stars. Marriage proposals, weddings, graduations, and many other occasions have been celebrated under starlight.

Karen's dad never painted stars on her ceiling as he promised, but her heavenly Father led her to another star. One Sunday the week before Christmas when Karen was ten years old, she visited a friend's church and saw a manger scene depicting the birth of Christ. It included the star of Bethlehem, shining over the manger. Looking at that star sparked a truth in Karen's heart, and God reassured her that her search for Him was not in vain. Karen could not count on a father's protection, but on that Sunday, she realized she now had a heavenly Father who would keep her safe.

> The LORD will keep you from all harm—he will watch over your life; the LORD will watch over your coming and going both now and forevermore.
> —Psalm 121:7–8

FOLLOWING IS A STORY of another little girl, Karen's sister, who also suffered silently. One afternoon after a crime was committed in her home, the police arrived. Hysterical tears, questions, and angry words spun around 7-year-old Diane like a giant spider web, weaving confusion, fear, and shame into her young heart. What had happened? What did that man do to her 14-year-old sister? Silently, she watched and listened, her big brown eyes reflecting the pain. If anyone had taken a moment to notice, they would have seen the hurt etched across her cherubic face.

Silently Suffering
Diane Wagner

For a seven-year-old, I had a lot of heavy stuff going on in my head. Ever since the afternoon the stranger came to our house, my life had changed. The police said a crime had occurred. I didn't totally understand, but I did remember my sister's shaky voice as she came up the stairs and said, "That man hurt me. We must go for help. Hurry! Hurry before he comes back!" Her hair was messed up, her clothes were on crooked, and tears streamed down her face. Looking at her made me afraid.

After that afternoon I couldn't even sleep in the same room with my sister, so I slept on the couch in our den. But its proximity to our parents' room presented problems, too, so I dreaded going to bed.

Wounded by Words

"Diane, its time to go to bed," Mom called. Dressed in my pajamas I climbed between the sheets. Then Mom kissed me good night. I rolled over and tried to go to sleep, but then the shouting began. *Why do Mom and Dad hate each other?* My thoughts swirled as I covered my head with my pillow to try and muffle the sound of their yelling.

"I need you at the shop all day!" Dad shouted.

"What's wrong with me coming to work after Richard's Boy Scout meeting?"

"Why can't Marilyn help with the meeting?" Dad persisted.

"Because it's not part of our babysitter's job."

"I need you at work!"

"Karen and I needed you at the police lineup! Diane went to that lineup and picked out the man who hurt Karen. Where were you?" Mom shouted back.

I squeezed my eyes shut trying to will myself to go to sleep, but instantly an image of the stranger's face appeared, along with the ashen facial features of my 14-year-old sister, Karen.

I thought back to what had happened. I had started to follow the man and my sister downstairs into our family room.

"Diane, please take our dog back upstairs so the man can measure the family room floor," my sister had insisted. After moving the dog out of the man's way, I had joined my brothers who were watching cartoons.

I didn't understand what had taken place that afternoon, but I felt guilty. Gone forever were my dreamy fantasies—a world of make-believe and magic. Through fairy tales like "Little Red Riding Hood and the Big Bad Wolf" or "Cinderella" I had been able to let my imagination soar. Not anymore. No fear existed for those mystical villains, but fear was very real in my world.

No one realized that I had become a child trapped in the middle of tragedy—my sister's rape. My childlike laughter stopped, my tears refused to flow, and my feelings inside had no words. *It must be my fault something bad happened to Karen,* I thought over and over.

My guilt grew like a monster whose tentacles sank deeper and deeper into my heart, isolating me, torturing me. Days and weeks turned into months, and the anger in our home became a suffocating blanket. Even my sister yelled at me more. Mom and Dad would fight, then suddenly stop and look at me. I believed it was because they blamed me for what had happened to my sister.

The unrealistic blame I carried in my heart as a little girl was a horrendous burden that I took into adulthood. A few years ago, I finally told Karen. "I blamed myself for what happened to you. I should have stayed with you—then maybe that man wouldn't have hurt you."

"Diane, you were just a little girl. You had no control over what happened to me. It was not your fault." With those words my long pent-up tears flowed, and I knew I'd been set free. Karen and I share a much closer relationship today.

● ● ●

A child needs to know as much information as is age appropriate. This is what should have been said: "Diane, a bad man hurt your sister, and all of us are very upset and angry over it. We dearly love both you and Karen and want to protect you. Neither of you is to blame for anything—only the horrible man. Our family will need to show each other a lot of love until we all get better."

If a young child wants details, it is better to say, "This is something we will talk about when you are older. We will tell you everything you want to know at that time."

Since children internalize pain and do not understand or have adequate coping skills and defense mechanisms, we must listen sincerely to their fears and provide a sense of security.

Diane fell under the post-traumatic stress disorder (PTSD) diagnosis, as possibly did Karen.

The description of post-traumatic stress disorder from the DSM-IV® manual, American Psychiatric Association is this:

Wounded by Words

The person has been exposed to a traumatic event in which:

1. The person experienced, witnessed, or was confronted with an event or events that involved actual or threatened death or serious injury, or a threat to the physical integrity of self or others.
2. The person's response involved intense fear, helplessness, or horror. Note: In children, this may be expressed instead by disorganized or agitated behavior.

The manual also lists disturbing effects. For PTSD victims, federal money is available for counseling in the Victims of Crime Fund (http://www.ojp.usdoj.gov/ovc/publications/factshts/vocacvf/welcome.html.).

Inside Friend
Connie L. Peters

There's a little brat inside of me
Who ridicules and derides me.
She calls me names,
Plays mind games,
Until I feel like screaming.

I wish she were a friend of mine,
Encouraging words all the time—
Showing respect and grace,
A cheerful face,
And support in my dreaming.

SHE WAS DRESSED for success—a professional woman, working at a major corporation and holding a high-level position as a manager. Her outward appearance indicated that she had it all together. No one would suspect she was falling apart on the inside.

Angel

Dr. Mary M. Simms

She had endured emotional abuse as a child and a ten-year marriage to an abusive spouse. However, as we dug deeper into her personal life, she reported that she had been in several emotionally abusive relationships since her divorce.

At the point when she came to me, seeking professional counseling, Angel was visibly broken and expressed her pain openly. "Is there something wrong with me? Why do I always attract emotionally abusive men? Is there a sign on my forehead that says 'I'm broken and available to abuse'"?

"No," I replied, "but let's explore your background to see if we can get some answers."

"I grew up in a home with constant conflict and verbal put-downs. I can hear my dad's voice in my head as if it were yesterday. He said, 'You're just like your mother, always making excuses for why things are not done. You're not smart, because you do things just like your mother does them—incomplete! You'd better work hard, or you won't get anyone to marry you!'"

Describing her experience caused Angel to burst into tears. For the first time she began to see a pattern of needing to please her dad and yet never receiving acceptance from him. There was never any affirmation for a job well done.

Further information on Angel's family history revealed an imbalance in her family system. Angel reported, "Mom tried to provide the emotional and physical needs of the entire family, six girls and one boy. My dad's work often kept him away, and when he came home he never seemed in the mood to interact with us, anyway. He often scolded Mom for things that he did not see accomplished."

Angel tearfully recalled a significant traumatic incident that had occurred when she was a little girl. "I remember one time Mom had all of us clean the house from stem to stern while she cooked a special dinner for Dad. Then we all dressed up. When my dad came home, Mom had us lined up to greet him with smiling faces. I will never forget that he screamed at us, saying, 'Go to your rooms. I don't need to be attacked when I come home!'

"Mom became angry and expressed her feelings. 'You're not acting appropriately toward us. We worked hard to make things special for you.'"

I interrupted Angel for a moment. "Did your mom's anger feel empowering?"

Angel answered, "Yes, very much so. I felt so much hate toward my dad at that moment that I actually felt strong when Mom confronted him." She sighed and then continued, "That feeling of strength did not last long though because he became enraged at Mom and yelled, 'You are undermining my parenting role in front of the children!' Then to make matters worse, he noticed that Mom was dressed in a fancier outfit than usual. He shouted, 'Why are you wearing something fancy in the house? You know you shouldn't wear good clothes to do household chores because they cost too much money. And besides, you look fat in that outfit!'"

Angel sighed. "My dad never told me or my sisters that we were pretty, either. No matter what we did, we couldn't fully meet his expectations."

Angel grew up building anger toward her dad, but did not realize that the anger she carried, as well as her low self-esteem and feelings of powerlessness in that home, would affect the decisions in her future relationships.

Her husband constantly put her down and placed unrealistic expectations on her just like her dad had. When she did not achieve the standards that her husband set for her, he complained, withheld love, and made condescending statements about her. She found herself trying to perform, to reach up to her husband's standards just as she had tried to do with her father. Angel started to develop a stress-related medical condition. Eventually, the marriage died when she found out that her husband was having an affair.

Two years after the divorce, Angel realized that if she wanted to attract a different kind of person, she needed to change her thinking about herself, and this is when she came to my office.

Part of the healing process for Angel required her to recognize that her low self-esteem had greatly contributed to choosing unhealthy relationships. Once she realized that her identity was wrapped up with feelings of unworthiness and victimization, she could then take ownership of these feelings and surrender them to the Lord Jesus Christ.

For Angel, the recovery process involved looking at the way she believed and how these beliefs were tied to her choices in relationships. On the surface, she did not see herself as powerless or victimized. However, she chose relationships where she became victimized and oppressed, because of the emotional abuse and programming that she experienced as a child. Angel recreated victimization in her own life by becoming a victim in the relationships she chose. And, as therapy progressed, she realized that on an unconscious level, she had not felt that she deserved better.

Angel first needed to learn the truth about herself and then how to replace the lies of her past with the truth, power, and integrity of God's Word. This involved learning to think differently about herself. She needed to see herself the way God saw her, fearfully and wonderfully made, with value. Psalm 139:13–14 states, *"For you created my inmost being; you knit me together in my mother's womb. I praise you because I am fearfully and wonderfully made; your works are wonderful. I know that full well."*

It also required active reprogramming. Angel developed a vital and active personal relationship with Christ, one that opened her eyes to the truth about her family of origin and the messages that helped to shape her thinking. As she spent time in meditation and Bible study, she began to see the integrity and character of God's love, which helped greatly to release her from the guilt and shame from her past. Once that release happened, she had new tools to erase the negative images that had reinforced her victimization messages. This enabled her to look at herself honestly, so she could acknowledge and surrender her negative emotions to God's control.

Finally, the last step was to practice using her new tools. Practice involved testing her skills to see if she had developed new eyes and understanding to attract healthier relationships. As she began to see herself differently, she was able to develop a new definition of what it meant to be in a healthy relationship. As she allowed the transforming power of God's grace and love to change her thinking, she began to make better relationship choices for herself.

After working with me for about one year, Angel terminated therapy. Approximately two years later, she reported that her new skills and faith in God had resulted in life-changing attitudes in these areas:
- Empowerment and strength
- Ability to seek a permanent, covenant relationship
- Desire to wait for the right person

● ● ●

In her former career as a high school counselor, Jeenie had the extra duty assignment of judging track. One afternoon, she was assigned to the pole-vaulters. Fascinated, she watched the boys plant their feet in the sand, grab the long pole, and hurl themselves over the bar. In practice, they began by setting the bar at a low level, and after much work, they achieved the height. Then, they raised the bar.

One young man said, "I started out putting the bar only a few feet above the ground, and now I have continued to raise the bar and reached heights I would never have dreamed."

These boys only raised the bar when they had achieved a certain height. They allowed themselves to experience the thrill of success at each new level.

Angel's father, however, raised the bar on his kids just before they came close to meeting his standards. Just as they were ready to scale the height, he raised his expectations so that no matter what they did, they never measured up. As a controller, he would not allow them to be successful. Failure was his forté. It was how he kept his family in check.

Promises are declarations that something will or will not be done. Broken promises by a friend or relative create mistrust. Once this bond is broken, we no longer rely on their word. *Deceit* in *Random House Webster Universal Dictionary* is defined as "intentional concealment or misrepresentation of the truth."

We find an example of deceit in Genesis 29 and 30. The love story of Jacob and Rachel is intertwined with a pretext— one that changed the lives of three people forever. Rachel is described as beautiful. When Jacob fell in love with Rachel he agreed to work for her father, Laban, for seven years. Jacob entered into that agreement in good faith, only to be deceived.

When the time arrived for Rachel to become his wife, the night air was filled with merriment. Jacob's heart must have raced with excitement. Innocently, he stood next to the woman who would soon become his wife. However, Laban had secretly replaced Rachel with his eldest daughter, Leah.

How did Laban manage to deceive Jacob? It is believed that Leah wore a heavy veil. Don't you wonder what thoughts raced through Leah's mind? *What will Jacob say when he looks upon me in the morning? I know it is Rachel he has worked for, Rachel he loves.*

Can you imagine the shock Jacob must have felt when he discovered the woman he'd shared the wedding bed with was Leah, not Rachel?

In Genesis 29 Jacob confronted Laban, asking, *"What is this you have done to me? I served you for Rachel, didn't I? Why have you deceived me?"* (v. 25).

Laban answered, *"It is not our custom here to give the younger daughter in marriage before the older one. Finish this daughter's bridal week; then we will give you the younger one also, in return for another seven years of work"* (vv. 26–27).

A person might believe that Leah also had reason to be angry at her father for putting her in a difficult position over which she had no control.

When Leah became pregnant for the first time she said, "It is because the LORD has seen my misery. Surely my husband will love me now" (v. 32). It's obvious to see that she continued to seek Jacob's love because each time she became pregnant, she made a similar comment and hoped that Jacob would finally love her.

God blessed the union between Jacob and Leah. Ultimately, she bore him six sons and a daughter. Genesis 30:14–15 says:

> *During wheat harvest, Reuben went out into the fields and found some mandrake plants [aphrodisiacs], which he brought to his mother Leah. Rachel said to Leah, "Please give me some of your son's mandrakes."*
>
> *But she said to her, "Wasn't it enough that you took away my husband? Will you take my son's mandrakes too?"*
>
> *"Very well," Rachel said, "he can sleep with you tonight in return for your son's mandrakes."*
> —Genesis 30:14–15

Events like this had to affect Leah's self-esteem. Can you imagine her watching Jacob go into Rachel's tent night after night? She probably heard them laughing and talking. How lonely she must have felt as she longed for Jacob to look at her with the love in his eyes that he showed toward Rachel! Yet, she knew that Rachel was his first and only love.

Even though Leah had a distorted image of herself, God loved and understood her in every way. Through His eyes, He saw her as perfect and complete. In 1 Corinthians 13:12 we read of looking in a mirror dimly, one that is indistinct, hazy, and unclear: *"Now we see but a poor reflection as in a mirror; then we shall see face to face. Now I know in part; then I shall know fully, even as I am fully known."*

Corinthian mirrors were made of highly polished brass. Though the mirrors were beautiful, the viewer was not able to see an accurate likeness of herself. Often we grab one of those ancient Corinthian mirrors and try to figure out who we are, based on the negative input of others.

God's creation is complete and perfect, and that is exactly how He sees us. God does not look at us as damaged goods, but as a divine work of art. There are no distorted images with Him.

Reflections

Write three negative thoughts that keep you from growing.

Lord, it's hard to reflect Your love when I feel so negative about myself. Help me to change my self-image.

CHAPTER 4

Sticks and Stones

I will instruct you and teach you in the way you
should go; I will counsel you and watch over you.
—Psalm 32:8

The old adage "Sticks and stones may break your bones, but names will never hurt you" is not true. Unkind words leave lasting scars, affecting how we deal with every aspect of our lives. An abused child, growing up in a dysfunctional home, will be the target of schoolyard bullies. Poor social skills aggravate this situation even more. A woman in a verbally abusive marriage may tend to withdraw, avoid social events, and become a recluse at work and even at church.

Many children also suffer emotional abuse at the hands of their classmates. This is especially true if they have a handicapping condition or something that sets them apart from their peers.

IN THE FOLLOWING STORY, Dandi Mackall tries to help her daughter, Katy, cope with the bullies at school.

Big Bad Bullies
Dandi Daley Mackall

I knew something was wrong as soon as my daughter, Katy, took her first step out of the school building. She hung her head, slipped into the car, and buckled her seat belt without being told.

"How was your day, Honey?" I asked cautiously.

"Fine."

Fifth grade's no picnic for any child, especially one who sticks out in class. And Katy has a rare neurological disorder that's impaired her hearing and speech. Katy's school days are seldom fine—and this day seemed less "fine" than most.

I started the car, the engine's rumble matching the churning inside me. As we left the parking lot in silence, Katy studied her backpack buckle.

I whispered a quick prayer, then asked, "Katy, what happened?"

Her words, and her tears, started spilling over. "Mitch stood behind me. He made fun of me. He talked funny—like me."

"Katy, I'm sorry," I said.

But Katy wasn't finished. "Then Melissa and Brianna laughed. They all laughed at me."

Katy cried harder.

I squeezed the steering wheel and said, "Katy, I love you so much, and I love the way you talk. Let's stop for ice cream on the way home."

● ● ●

It's tough in the school trenches. And if a student has a disability, as Katy does, it's that much harder. But even typical school-age children may find themselves targets of a bully.

My friend Linda's second-grade daughter gets teased for being overweight. Her fourth-grade son is ridiculed for wearing thick glasses. Another seventh-grader refuses to participate in sports because he's not a natural athlete. He can't stand the verbal abuse when he strikes out. And another friend's daughter, Nicole, struggles with assignments. She's been labeled slow or even stupid by several of her classmates. They think Nicole doesn't hear their whispers.

So what's a mother to do? We pray, get the facts, and do what God leads us to do. Then we admit there's only so much we can do about the bullies of this world. Our job is to prepare and teach our own children how to deal with them.

While you may never be able to change other people's kids, when you help your child endure tough experiences, he or she grows by learning important lessons about compassion, forgiveness, and comfort in God, as well as effective survival skills.

My friend Meg regrets that she lost opportunities to teach her daughter, Becky, how to face bullies. Meg's goal was to fix every problem so Becky wouldn't experience pain. If Becky got left out of an overnighter, Meg called the other mom and arranged for Becky to be included. If Becky got in trouble in high school, Meg was there to defend her daughter and get the consequences lessened. Now that Becky is away at college, Meg can't fix every problem. And Becky, sheltered from problems and pain for so many years, hasn't developed problem-solving skills to handle even minor struggles.

God didn't put us in a pain-free world. Romans 5:3–5 says pain and perseverance are parts of a character-building formula: *"Not only so, but we also rejoice in our sufferings, because we know that suffering produces perseverance; perseverance, character; and character, hope. And hope does not disappoint us, because God has poured out his love into our hearts by the Holy Spirit, whom he has given us."*

If we can help our children handle bullies now, we'll equip them for a godly life later.

I wish I had a solution to the problem of Mitch teasing Katy. We prayed. My husband and I told Katy we loved her and Jesus loved her. We couldn't find an explanation for Mitch's behavior, but we prayed for him. We talked to Katy's teacher, who already was aware of the problem. She had her students switch desks, and Katy ended up several seats away from Mitch. It slowed him down, but it didn't stop him.

My husband and I coached Katy on how she could handle the situation if it came up again. We rehearsed. Dad was Mitch. Katy's sister and I were the other girls. In practice, Katy responded cheerfully to the pretend teasing. She said, "Have a nice day, Mitch. You, too, girls." Or, "Mitch, you want to come with me to speech therapy?"

Katy did fine—in practice. At school, she forgot her lines. The problem ended when the school year ended. This year, we hope she'll be a little better equipped.

Jeenie suggests that the technique used by the Mackalls to go back over the scenarios in which their daughter was bullied is an excellent one. A parent can go through the episode event by event to help the child determine what he or she could have said or done in the situation to stop the bullying. Then, the parents can role-play each occurrence until the child becomes more adept at understanding the numerous ways the event could have been handled.

On the other hand, oversheltering a child can cause even more problems. Jeenie will never forget the Brown family at the high school where she counseled. Robbie, an incoming ninth-grader, came into her office with his mother and huddled in the corner while his mother proceeded to tell Jeenie how the school should be run and what she needed to do for Robbie. That mother had four children, and year after year, she returned to the counseling office over some silly incident Jeenie needed to rectify. All four of her children were bullied by their peers and never learned to stand up for themselves.

Rescuing our kids can become a deadly habit that will greatly handicap them in their adult lives. It can easily set them up for marrying a controller, because they feel comfortable in that setting—just like home.

Bully stories don't always have happy endings. Yet with Christ's help, no matter what other people's children do, our children can grow in character and strength—and we can grow with them.

ALTHOUGH KATY AND the Brown children didn't find an easy solution to stopping their classmates from teasing them, in the following story, Sharon succeeded in accomplishing this. Through much prayer, she worked up the nerve to face her classmates and tell them why her eyes were different colors.

When the Blind See

Karen Kosman

A recent phone call ushered in the excited voice of my best friend. "We are the proud grandparents of a new grandson!"

As little girls Sharon and I played with our dolls; today we exchange stories of our grandchildren. After I hung up from our phone conversation I thought back to our childhood years.

The first time I met Sharon, she walked into my third-grade classroom as a new student, and Mrs. Tanner announced, "Class, this is Sharon. Please make her feel welcome."

Sharon looked down at the floor and smiled. She wore a bright red pinafore with white polka dots and a white blouse. She looked fragile like a fine china doll with her dark, curly hair and creamy white complexion. From where I sat, I couldn't see the color of her eyes.

Suddenly, a faint snicker spread around the room. Sharon looked up startled, and we made eye contact. I smiled, and she smiled back. I noticed that her eyes looked different, but I didn't know why.

"Thank you, Sharon. Now you can take your seat—the empty one over there," Mrs. Tanner said. My heart raced with excitement because the empty seat was in front of mine.

Good, I thought, *I can't wait until lunch, and then we can talk.* But when we were finally dismissed for lunch, Sharon quickly exited the door. I tried to follow her, but she met with a boy, taller and older than she. As they walked away toward the cafeteria, I wondered who he was. Later I found out Bobby was her older brother.

Every day he met her outside our classroom and walked her to the cafeteria. Then one day Bobby didn't show up. As soon as Sharon went into the hallway, a group of boys from our class approached her. They pointed at her and laughed, chanting, "Two-eyed freak, two-eyed freak." Sharon quickly pushed her way through them without saying a word and walked away. She didn't let them see the tears in her eyes.

I ran over to her and asked, "Would you like to have lunch with me?"

For a moment I thought she was going to walk away, but she said, "OK."

"I saw what those boys did to you and heard what they said. Don't pay any attention to them. They always act dumb."

"I'm used to kids teasing me because of my eyes. I'm blind in one eye, so that's why my eyes are different colors."

"What happened? Were you in an accident?"

"No, when I was one year old I had the chicken pox, and then the measles soon after that. Those illnesses left me blind in my left eye."

From that day forward Sharon and I were best friends. We lived close enough to each other that we could get together in the afternoons after school. The attic in Sharon's house became a safe place to play with our dolls. As we climbed the old wooden steps, they emitted a musical creaking sound.

"I bet I can reach the top without making the stairs creak," I said laughing.

"No one has been able to do that," Sharon replied just as a loud creaking noise erupted from beneath my foot. We both broke out in hysterical laughter.

I still have fond memories of the attic's musty smell and of dust particles dancing on beams of sunlight streaming through the small window.

At school the teasing and taunting continued. Then one day Bobby got in a fight with a boy named Tom, who was harassing Sharon. Bobby and Tom were called into the principal's office along with their parents. After all the reasons for the fight were discussed, Sharon's dad stood up and said, "My son has been taught to protect his sister. He should not have hit Tom, but then Tom should not tease my daughter. So that's the end of it." Then he got up and walked out with Bobby.

Soon after that incident Sharon bravely, with the help of Mrs. Tanner, stood in front of our class and explained why her eyes were different.

"Some of you have brown eyes, some green, and some blue. I was born with two brown eyes, but now I have one green eye and one brown." Sharon paused and looked right at her tormentors and said, "But that does not make me a freak. I've been blind in my left eye since I was a baby. I had the chicken pox and measles and almost died. Going blind made my left eye turn green."

"Thank you, Sharon. You're very brave to share with us."

The teasing stopped after that. Our whole third-grade class learned a lesson. We all learned that courage and truth are powerful. Sharon's talk made a statement to the bullies— who were truly the blind ones.

● ● ●

Jeenie states that few children are brave enough to stand in front of a classroom and explain their deformity as did Sharon. Nor should they be encouraged or expected to do so. The teacher, Mrs. Tanner, missed a valuable teaching moment when Sharon became one of her students. She was aware on the first day, when she looked into Sharon's eyes, that Sharon would become the target of abuse. The snickering in the classroom confirmed her suspicion, but at first she did nothing to stop it.

It would have been wise for Mrs. Tanner to explain the situation to the principal and ask that Sharon be called into the office the next day to be welcomed by the principal in order to give Mrs. Tanner time to talk to her students. It was the teacher's responsibility, not Sharon's, to explain Sharon's blindness to the class. Mrs. Tanner needed to state that any unkindness would not go unpunished.

When Jeenie was faced with a similar situation, she handled it differently. One day a student fresh from Vietnam entered her classroom. Trang could barely speak English and certainly did not fit the picture of a typical freshman. The taunts began.

The next day, Jeenie requested Trang be called out of class for a few minutes. While he was gone, she reiterated the story of how he and his siblings escaped from Vietnam in a small aircraft. For a few moments, their parents hung to the bottom of the plane, with tears streaming down their faces. Jumping to the ground, they watched as their children were airlifted to safety—never to be seen again.

Although there was not a dry eye in the classroom, Jeenie threatened big-time discipline if she heard of any abuse regarding Trang. The classmates opened their hearts of compassion to him, and four years later, Jeenie watched them all graduate as friends.

BOTH MRS. TANNER and Jeenie realized the problem at hand and helped to solve it, but the mother in the following story was not so discerning.

"But I'm So Thirsty!"
Bonnie Compton Hanson

On a recent holiday I found myself in an overflowing walk-in emergency clinic. Apparently half the town had managed to come down with an injury or illness on this long weekend. Broken bones, pulled ligaments, bronchitis, sniffles, stomach flu—you name it—someone in the room was suffering from it.

My own complaint was an infected spider bite. I wallowed in self-pity until I heard crying in the chair directly behind me.

Turning around, I saw a sad little girl, about five or six years old. Seated next to her was an older sister. Next to the older sister sat the mother. The older sister was busy with a Game Boy. The mother was talking loudly to someone on her cell phone—even though such phones were banned inside the medical facility.

The little girl kept whimpering, "I'm so thirsty, Mommy. Could I please have something to drink? I'm so thirsty. Could I please have something to drink?" Her face was flushed, her eyes dull, and obviously, she was running a high fever. No mother could keep from worrying about her and rushing to help her—except this woman.

"Shut up!" she yelled at her younger daughter. "I'm on the phone. Shut up and quit your whining. Quit it, I say!"

"But, Mommy," sobbed the child. "Just a drink of water, please? I'm so thirsty. Please, Mommy, just a drink?"

"I'm warning you, crybaby!" her mother snarled. "You stupid kid! One more peep out of you, and I'm taking you back home without the doctor seeing you. Then you'll be sorry!"

Horrified, I stood up to get the child a drink myself. But I was too late. Yanking both daughters by their arms—and still talking on her cell phone—the furious woman pulled them right out of their seats and pushed them out the front door. And they did not return.

● ● ●

Yes, children often make too much noise. They screech, giggle, yell, and complain. Sad, mad, or glad, they are impossible not to *hear*.

But *listening* to them is an entirely different matter. Yes, we parents get irritable and exhausted, and we worry over what we consider to be "more important" matters. Yet, we should never be too preoccupied to listen to our little ones—with not just our ears, but our hearts also.

That little girl was learning a sad lesson—that no matter what, even in an emergency, she had to keep quiet. Only her mother was allowed to speak. Otherwise, the child faced a torrent of verbal abuse. Such treatment could not only break her heart, but endanger her life.

God doesn't forbid His children from speaking to Him; indeed, He encourages it. How can we parents do less?

During 20 years as a school counselor, Jeenie often heard the words, "My parents don't listen to me." She asked God to give counsel to the parents of these students as well as to direct her in this area of her life as a mother.

The technique God brought to mind is for parents to sit on the floor with each child ten minutes a day and *listen*. No talking. Keep quiet and hear what the child has to say.

While sitting on the floor, the parent is eye to eye with the child, close enough to touch, and there are no outside distractions. Other family members know when a parent is on the floor, he or she is off limits to everyone else.

After attending one of Jeenie's speaking engagements, one parent stated, "I heard you give this concept over a year ago. Both my husband and I practice it daily, and it has revolutionized our home."

THE FOLLOWING STORY portrays a teacher who did not practice Jeenie's technique. She bullied and threatened until one of her students ran away from school.

"I'll Never Run Away Again"
Karen Kosman

I knew I hadn't done well. We'd just finished our spelling test. My fourth-grade teacher, Mrs. Hamstring, walked over to my desk. She looked angry. Pulling me up by my arms she said, "Karen, you didn't study. If you had, you wouldn't have missed so many words."

"I did study, but…"

"Don't make matters worse by lying," she said sternly. "At recess you'll write each misspelled word eight times on the blackboard."

I felt my face flush, and inside I thought, *I did study; I tried hard.* But I knew by the look on her face that it wouldn't do any good to try to defend myself. She'd already made her judgment. When she let go of me, I sat back down. I lay my head down in my arms on my desk so my classmates wouldn't see me crying. It was bad enough to hear angry words at home, let alone come to school and have my teacher angrily accuse me of lying. *Why is she always so mean to me in front of the other kids?* I thought, feeling overwhelmed and confused.

Later at home, when Mom asked about the bruises on my arms I made up a story. I didn't tell Mom about my school problems because she had enough to deal with at home. I told myself that I'd do better in school. But another part of me didn't believe I could improve.

The following Friday as our school bus parked, my terrified mind pleaded, *Dear God, I can't take the spelling test.*

It wasn't always easy to study at home, especially if Dad had been drinking. Such had been the case the previous night. I had tried to study in my closet with the light on and the door closed to drown out Dad's yelling.

As I got off the school bus, I felt sick to my stomach. Instead of going to my classroom I ran to the school office. I thought, *Maybe I can convince the nurse that I'm really sick, and she will send me home.*

There I found my girlfriend, Toni, who was returning to school after being sick for a week. "Karen, why are you here?"

"I don't want to take the spelling test," I whispered.

"I don't want to be here, either."

"Why don't we just leave," I whispered. Slipping off our chairs we quietly exited the office. Outside we ran and didn't stop until we reached the bus stop. We each had our change ready for the city bus. Once we were on the bus we wondered how we'd explain coming home early.

"Let's get off at the shopping center," Toni whispered.

"OK. Then we can take a later bus home."

We hid our lunch boxes under some bushes and went into a ladies room where we tried to disguise ourselves. Toni braided my pigtails, and I put her ponytail in a bun. Feeling grown-up, we left the restroom. When the store clerks questioned why we were out of school, Toni explained, "Ve're fom Germany und wisiting width friends."

But soon our world of make-believe came crashing down when a neighbor, who had volunteered to look for us, found us.

Mr. Nickoloff said, "Karen, your friend Sharon told your teacher she'd seen you at school. When your lunch boxes were returned to school, the police were called. They thought you'd been kidnapped."

We climbed into the backseat of his car. Toni and I huddled close together, too scared to speak. Back at school my pregnant mom was sitting in a police car. Her face was red and swollen from crying, but she hugged me and said, "I'm so glad you're both safe. Please don't ever do this again."

In the principal's office I had to face Mrs. Hamstring. I broke down and confessed, "I was too scared to take the spelling test. I didn't want Mrs. Hamstring to get mad at me." But I didn't tell them the whole story. Mrs. Hamstring looked away from me. I wondered if she felt sorry.

After that afternoon my teacher never lost her temper again with me, and I learned to face my fears. My punishment came from knowing how much I'd hurt Mom, the one person I knew loved me. I promised, "I'll never run away again."

● ● ●

Two wrongs don't make a right. We need to teach our children to tell someone if they are being abused in any form. Running away seemed like the right solution, but it only resulted in more pain. Karen's actions hurt someone she loved.

Life is full of choices. Even in a child's life, God uses those choices, right or wrong, to teach and correct. Even though Karen felt afraid when she faced her teacher in the principal's office, she found strength in expressing her feelings, and she drew comfort from her mother's love. She made a promise to never run away again.

A quote by Horace Mann states, "The teacher who is attempting to teach without inspiring the pupil with a desire to learn is hammering on cold iron."

Sticks and Stones
Connie L. Peters

Sticks and stones
Can break my bones
But words will never hurt me.
The truth of this little rhyme
Truly does desert me.

It's true I need not receive them.
Their power is in how I perceive them.
But words can be like flaming arrows
Not breaking bones but
Piercing marrow.

Words like slave drivers' hands
Bind with constraining bands,
Keeping us from what God intended—
Trapped, controlled
Abused, and offended.
There is a Word, His name is Jesus.
He's the one who truly frees us
From our constructed prisons.
Instead of death, He speaks life,
If we would only listen.

An example of verbal abuse by one brother to another is found in 1 Samuel 17. David's father asked him to take ten loaves of bread and an ephah (a bushel) of roasted grain to his brothers' camp. He said, *"See how your brothers are and bring back some assurance from them. They are with Saul and all the men of Israel in the Valley of Elah, fighting against the Philistines"* (vv. 18–19).

When David reached the camp, he greeted his brothers. While he was talking to them, Goliath, the nine-foot-tall Philistine, stepped forward and hurled insults, challenging the Israelites to send someone to fight him. Not only did his height threaten them, but his attire sent a message, too: *Don't mess with me, or I'll crush you.* Obviously this giant warrior, wearing bronze armor and a helmet and carrying a bronze javelin on his back, put fear in the hearts of the Israelites. They turned and ran.

David watched the scenario and asked, "What will be done for the man who kills this Philistine and removes this disgrace from Israel?" (v. 26). He was told that Israel would be free of the Philistines if one of the Israelite soldiers defeated the giant.

> *When Eliab, David's oldest brother, heard him speaking with the men, he burned with anger at him and asked, "Why have you come down here? And with whom did you leave those few sheep in the desert? I know how conceited you are and how wicked your heart is; you came down here only to watch the battle."*
>
> *"Now what have I done?" said David. "Can't I even speak?"*
>
> —1 Samuel 17:28–29

David's reaction to the caustic words of his brother was to turn away and talk to somebody else. In essence, he just ignored his brother's comments.

Who would expect God to use a shepherd boy to slay a giant? What a sight it must have been—a formidable giant coming against a young shepherd whose only weapons were a sling and a rock. Yet, Goliath toppled over, fatally wounded by David's stone.

God chose a shepherd whose incredible faith towered over the giant Philistine. In time David became king of Israel, and God called him *"a man after his own heart"* (1 Samuel 13:13–14 and Acts 13:22).

Smart man, that David. He refused to be a victim of Eliab's taunts and accusations. David did not cower, but responded back in truth, then turned to talk to someone else—ending the confrontation.

What an example for us when we are unjustly accused! We can either choose to be the injured party, or confront the issue kindly and firmly. In other words, we can speak the truth in love and not allow ourselves to be the butt of someone's dysfunction. Then we can walk away from it.

Many times Jeenie has suggested to her clients in therapy that when the perpetrator starts mouthing off, the client should give a short rebuttal and then leave the room. David's rebuttal consisted of only nine words. When you face circumstances like these, do not stand around, waiting for more emotional volcanic ash to bury you.

Undoubtedly, David understood the underlying issues of his oldest brother. Even though he did not confront them, he knew what he was dealing with. Eliab looked at David through green eyes of jealousy. Likely, he knew David was already anointed to be the next king of Israel and that someday he would bow his knee in allegiance to his baby brother. So he showed disrespect toward David, treating him as a spoiled brat.

Eliab probably knew David had protected his sheep numerous times. On one occasion he had grabbed a lion by the beard and killed it, and another time he had killed a bear. Word had gotten around that David was a man of courage, as well as an excellent marksman who never missed the target.

Hatred oozed from Eliab's inner being. Thus, it was imperative in his mind that he tear down David's accomplishments, as well as his commitment to God.

We all have encountered Eliabs in our lives—people who are vicious and will do whatever they can to destroy and wound our spirits. So often, they succeed. How tragic.

Sticks and stones may break our bones, but so do caustic words—breaking our inner selves. When verbal stones are hurled toward us, we need to get out of the way. Then we can turn the stones meant for evil around and use them for good. We can stand on faith, seek help, speak the truth, educate others, and share the hope we have found in God.

Describe a time when a bully called you names and made you a target of ridicule.

Lord, when I'm a target of those who degrade me, help me to disregard their lies.

CHAPTER 5

Telltale Signs

For he has not despised or disdained
the suffering of the afflicted one;
he has not hidden his face from him
but has listened to his cry for help.
—Psalm 22:24

We try to ignore thoughtless comments and insults, but often they seem like a dripping faucet. We may disregard them for a while, but like the faucet, the sound becomes louder and louder until we can no longer ignore it. If the verbal abuse continues, our foundation is slowly eroded until it collapses.

We desperately search for an escape, but questions such as *Where would I go? Who'd believe me?* entrap us. Victims of verbal abuse find it difficult to ask for the help they desperately need. They struggle with doubts: *Who cares, anyway? No one would understand. It's my fault. I can't tell anyone because it is too embarrassing.*

A vicious cycle is formed, which can affect our faith and cause us to move away from God. This often leads to poor choices and negative attitudes as the person suffers silently. Because victims often cover up for what is going on in the home, at school, or in the workplace, they struggle with self-respect. The following scenario may describe someone you know, or perhaps your own situation.

At a friend's birthday celebration, Mary and her husband mingle among the other guests. Suddenly, Mary's cheeks turn bright red, she has trouble breathing, and her palms become sweaty. Mark had vowed that he'd never belittle her again in front of friends and family. His promise echoes in her mind. *I'm sorry, Mary. I'll never criticize you again.*

How could he forget that promise? Tears threaten to fall. No one seems to notice, or maybe they just don't care. Heartbroken, Mary excuses herself and rushes to the ladies room where she attempts to cover up her flushed face with more makeup.

"Counseling is helping," she whispers. "At least that's what I thought last week."

But just moments earlier her husband's criticism had crushed her hopes. Standing with a group of friends he'd boldly stated, "My wife sure needs me. Mary can't balance our checkbook. She doesn't even know how to turn on the computer."

God, where are You? Mary questions. *Am I that needy? Why does he constantly ridicule me? If he loves me, why does he make me the center of his sick humor?*

Mary returns to the party and walks over to a good friend. When she tries to explain what just happened, her friend gives her a condescending smile and says, "You could do worse. Maybe if you try harder or lose weight, things will get better."

Mary walks away without saying another word. She goes directly to the buffet and finds comfort in the bite-sized pizzas and chips and dip. She'll start her diet again tomorrow. Maybe. For now, Mary suffers silently.

Jeenie suggests that even though Mary's husband was out of line, Mary chose to be devastated. Feeling that she had no recourse with her spouse, she ran to her friend, who turned out to be rather like Job's friends—caustic. When that didn't work, she crammed food into her mouth, but that wasn't the solution, either.

Wounded by Words

Notice the chain of unhealthy events: a disrespectful husband; an uncaring friend; and finally, the one thing that made her feel better—at least for the moment—food.

Mary stuffed her feelings by feeding her face, but actually, eating added to her low self-esteem. She would soon feel ashamed of popping unhealthy food into her mouth. It was a downward spiral—likely, one she repeated often.

In our American culture, food is one of our most reliable comforters. We eat when we're depressed, happy, sad, or angry. It's a mood changer—for about ten minutes.

Moms often began the practice, thinking they were acting out of love. "I'm so sorry the kids made fun of you at school. Here's a cookie." Or, "Let me bandage your bleeding knee, then we'll get ice cream." No wonder we choose food as the method to satisfy our inner longings.

A better choice for Mary would have been to stand up for herself in a kind but firm way. Perhaps she might have used a bit of humor to deflate the unkind slur.

For instance, Mary could have said, "Well, I guess I have a lot of company in not being perfect. Or then, again, maybe I should just be shot." The group would likely have laughed at such a bizarre statement, and the remark would be forgotten. Mary's self-worth would have jumped up a notch. If she continued to practice this technique, it wouldn't be long before her husband would discontinue the discourteous verbiage. He would soon learn Mary wasn't going to let him off the hook—ever.

We have a choice whether we accept unkind, cruel words or not. Just because they are hurled at us doesn't mean we need to stand there and be smacked in the face. There is always the possibility of ducking.

It will take constant practice to come up with short phrases to counterbalance cruel remarks. And practice we must, if we intend to be the emotionally healthy individuals God intended.

Ugly Paint
Connie L. Peters

One of my best friends said
Something thoughtless, Lord, and
Hurt my feelings.
I shared something personal and
Requested prayer.
Her reply of condemnation
Cut me to the quick.
Lord, help me forgive my friend for
Pronouncing judgment over me.
If there is some truth to what she says,
Show me the problem and how to solve it.
Help me treat her with
Respect and kindness, and
Be OK about who I am,
Even if she painted an ugly picture of me.

IN SIMILAR CIRCUMSTANCES as Mary's, Susan chose to give in to her husband to avoid further confrontation.

Piano Lessons
Susan Titus Osborn

My first husband accepted a one-year assignment in Washington, D.C., when the boys were in first and third grade. Richard, who was eight, had been playing the piano since he was five. We didn't want him to lose ground, so we had the piano hauled to McLean, Virginia, with our personal items.

I found a wonderful teacher for Richard, and since I had some extra time, I decided to take piano lessons, too. As a type-A personality, I tend to try to overachieve at everything, making it difficult to find things to do just for fun. It quickly became apparent that I had no musical talent, but I was having fun, doing something relaxing that I realized I would never become good at. I felt no pressure to achieve.

When we moved back to California, I continued taking piano lessons from a friend who was also teaching Richard. Again, I found it fun, and it gave me an appreciation for music and for the gifts of perfect pitch and nimble fingers that my oldest son possessed—gifts not given to me.

One day, I was practicing my simple little songs when my husband walked in. He listened for a moment, and then said, "You play terribly."

"I know," I agreed, and then added, "but I'm really having fun."

"I don't care if you're having fun. I want you to stop the lessons."

"Why? I really enjoy playing—"

He interrupted me midsentence. "It's a waste of your time and my money. End of discussion."

With those words, he stomped out of the living room.

A feeling of overpowering sadness filled my heart. I knew it wasn't a matter of money. He was an executive and made a good salary, and there was always enough money for his golf and flying lessons. I never resented his activities. Yet, he was very controlling, and when he made up his mind about something, no room remained for discussion. Plus, I didn't care enough about my piano lessons to go to war with my husband, and that is what it would have been to fight him on the subject.

I sighed and closed the piano lid. I put my music in the piano bench and never took it out again. That day, my piano-playing days ended, and I never mentioned my desire to play the piano ever again.

● ● ●

"That's how a controller is—controlling. The controller will hurt, damage, or pillage anyone who gets in his way. The only outcome he considers is what he wants," says Jeenie. "Susan's first husband was a perfect example of a narcissistic personality. In his sadistic way, he was out to destroy anything Susan or her children cherished. If it brought them pleasure, it was over.

"This manipulating husband was used to his family folding. Therefore, it didn't take much for him to get his evil way. No one bucked him. One of his controlling mechanisms was to make it so rough for people to stand up to him that they gave in rather than go through another big fight, which they would always lose.

"The best way to handle a narcissistic controller is keep your mouth shut, then do what you want. Susan could have continued to practice the piano when he was at work or enjoying one of his recreational pursuits, never bringing up the subject again."

Jeenie's advice to others like Susan is, "Open up that piano and follow your dream."

KAREN'S HUSBAND, JOHN, suffered silently for many years, without dealing with his invisible scars from childhood. First he joined the navy in hopes of escaping his past, but he couldn't run far or fast enough. During his 21-year first marriage, his past continued to haunt him. That devastation eventually brought him to a spiritual crossroad in his life where he accepted Christ as his Protector and Fortress.

"I'm Sorry God Put Breath in You"
John Kosman

I sat at the end of the jetty. The sand on the beach sparkled in the sun behind me, and the ocean waves seemed to beckon me. I'd always loved this beach. Yet, that afternoon my heart felt empty—I sat there wanting to put an end to my pain.

My 21-year marriage had ended, and I had moved into a one-bedroom apartment. I thought, *This is the end of the world. I've lost everything, my wife, my children, and my home.* I leaned forward thinking, *All I have to do is jump in and sink to the bottom.* This new crisis in my life opened old wounds from my childhood, and I bled once again.

As a teenager I'd experienced similar feelings of rejection. At school my coach, a man I admired, gave me the nickname "Skinny Bird Legs." My coach and teammates saw humor in name calling, but I was the one who felt the pain.

At 15, I was thin and self-conscious about my weight. Perhaps if this had been an isolated incident, it wouldn't have overwhelmed me. But a few days later, I came home from school late, and an argument with Mom ended in a final insult to my already damaged self-image.

"Just wait till your dad gets home," Mom yelled, "I'm sorry God put breath in you!"

Normally, when Mom threatened, "Just wait till your dad gets home," an encounter with Dad ensued in our basement. A beating with a belt was my punishment for something as minor as forgetting to take out the trash. The confusion, anger, and drinking in our home ate away at me like a cancer. I desperately wanted to cut out that cancer.

I held back tears as I thought, *I've always felt unwanted. Mom, you just proved I'm right. You don't care. Parties and drinking are all you and Dad live for.*

A short time later I stood at the top of the stairs in my parents' home wanting to end the loneliness. I thought, *I'm bad. I need to be punished. Maybe if I jump, Mom and Dad will pay attention.*

I threw myself down the stairs. Bruised and battered, I ached all over, and my right arm throbbed with pain. I continued to lay prostrate on the hard wooden floor. Then I heard Mom's scream, "Oh no! What happened? John, are you all right? I'll get your dad."

Mom rushed into the living room and told Dad what happened. He replied, "You deal with it," and he didn't even come into the hall to check me over. My parents didn't take me to the doctor. They did nothing.

My mind agonized. I thought, *They really don't care, so why should I care?*

The next day I returned to school with a badly sprained arm and bruises, but the real source of my pain went undiagnosed—verbal abuse.

Eventually I joined the navy, and the day I left for boot camp, Mom cried, "Your dad forced you to join the navy. Didn't he?"

"No, Mom; Dad didn't force me. I joined because I wanted to. I have to get away from all the crazy fighting between you and Dad."

"We don't fight that bad, do we?" she asked in amazement.

I didn't answer her, but I wondered how she could live in such denial. And I soon discovered that although I had managed to put an ocean between me and my family, I could not run from the pain inside.

Twenty-seven years after Mom made that comment, I sat on the jetty, thinking about my present situation. I watched the churning water swirl around the rocks. "God," I prayed, "I brought anger and jealousy into my marriage. I want my life to change. I want an end to the pain. Is there any chance to start life anew?"

Suddenly something caught my attention. I looked up and saw a sailboat with red, white, and blue sails powered by the wind. A voice within whispered, *John, keep sailing.* For the first time that day I felt the warmth of the sun and enjoyed the beauty that surrounded me. "Lord, I need You to be the skipper in my life, to guide me through life's storms."

Wounded by Words

Angry words flung carelessly like an arrow hit their target. Bull's-eye! Normally when an arrow hits the heart of its prey, death occurs. John's self-talk brought about disastrous choices. When we speak to each other, we do so at about 200 words a minute, but our self-talk is 1,300 words per minute. We tell ourselves lots of things—all day long.

When we are hurt and angry, most of our self-talk is pessimistic. Over and over in our minds we rehearse the entire situation—in great detail. We then become victimizers of ourselves. Negative, destructive self-talk can go on for years—a cancer, eating us inside out.

To become emotionally healthy, we must change our thought patterns. Whenever the negative thoughts come to mind, tell yourself, "I'm not going to think about it now." Perhaps use the command, "Stop it!" Then, turn your thoughts elsewhere by doing a task that is physical to help occupy your mind: take a walk; dig in the garden; exercise; or wash the car.

It is tedious and difficult to turn off and control our negative thoughts. At first, we may need to do it hundreds of times a day. As time progresses, however, it becomes easier. Eventually, it is no longer a major, controlling part of life.

God is able and willing to heal our damaged emotions, but we must work with Him by throwing out harmful thoughts and replacing them with affirming ones. Philippians 4:8 states: *"Whatever is true, whatever is noble, whatever is right, whatever is pure, whatever is lovely, whatever is admirable—if anything is excellent or praiseworthy—think about such things."*

THE FOLLOWING STORY tells of an eight-year-old girl who was emotionally traumatized by a teacher, yet suffered in silence. As an adult, Janet later accepted Jesus's love and forgiveness, which enabled her to forgive the teacher who had wronged her so many years before.

The Echo of Love
Janet Eckles

I sat in the back of the school bus, alone and quiet in my own world. The rest of the third grade girls giggled as they talked and teased each other. But I remained withdrawn, pretending to be entertained by the action in the streets of La Paz. My heart ached. I longed to laugh with them, but an episode two days prior still burned in my heart.

My mom had come home from work and given her usual greeting. "How's my little girl?"

I wanted to smile, but instead tears spilled down my cheeks.

"What's the matter, honey?" Mom bent over and cupped my face in her hands.

"I don't know." At first I feared telling Mom what happened. The words of my third-grade teacher, Sister Modesta, rang in my ears. I had made a mistake in reciting the memorized lesson. I stopped and looked at my teacher, knowing a scolding followed.

"Wipe that smirk off your face," she growled as she struck me with her open hand.

My face stung, but the blow didn't hurt as much as the humiliation. I felt all eyes in the room staring at me.

Mom's inquiries jolted me back to the present. "Did someone hurt you?"

Finally, I sighed and said softly. "Sister Modesta hit me. She slapped me."

"Why?" Mom sounded shocked.

"I missed part of the lesson, and she said I was smiling. She didn't like that."

Mom called my father's younger brother, a well-respected priest. She told him about the incident and asked if he could look into what happened. He agreed. No one told me what he said to Sister Modesta, nor did I ask.

The next day, my teacher displayed an even harsher tone than before. She walked into the classroom, stood behind her

Wounded by Words

desk, and before she took roll, she glared at me. "Quiet!" she commanded, hitting her desk with a ruler.

I tensed up. Her harsh words made my stomach cramp.

"Everybody," Sister Modesta called out to the class, "see Janet Perez over there?"

Everyone turned and stared at me. My teacher's tone startled me, but I knew I hadn't done anything wrong.

"Janet's a liar. She went home and told her parents that I hit her. Did anybody see me hit her?"

The class remained silent.

She rounded her desk and headed in my direction. "All of you are forbidden to play with her at recess. Anyone caught near her will be punished." She stood next to my desk and looming over me. Wearing her black habit, she snarled. "No one should be around liars."

Her words cut through me. The sound of her voice pierced my 8-year-old heart, and I trembled inside. At recess, I sat on the side, watching my classmates play as they ignored me. I vowed I'd never tell anyone anything that happened to me again. If I did, the consequences would be too painful.

From that moment on, I lived with the image of myself as a liar. My heart put up a barrier. The tender words coming from Mom's lips no longer held reassurance. I doubted her love. *How could she love a liar?*

The days that followed during the school year brought agonizing pain for me. I couldn't tell anyone of Sister Modesta's harsh words, directed to me every chance she got. I tried harder to do well on tests, memorization, and homework, but her words of ridicule when I made small mistakes crushed me.

As I grew up, the desire to perform, to please, and to bow to authority created anxiety within me. I spent all my energy attempting to prove I was worthy to be trusted. And times when I failed, I agonized, fearing I'd be labeled and rejected.

Then at the age of 32, I accepted Jesus as my Savior. The circumstances in which I made the decision were also painful and agonizing. I had begun to lose my sight. When my world turned dark in every sense, I looked up and invited Jesus to shine in my darkness.

He opened my spiritual eyes and softened my heart for me to hear His words of tenderness and acceptance. His Word also opened the path to freedom—the freedom of forgiveness. And although memories of Sister Modesta had faded, I chose to forgive her. And in contrast to the way my stomach once twisted because of her words, my soul now delights as Jesus's promises echo reassurance and unconditional love for me.

● ● ●

Eventually, after the anger and self-examination are done, forgiveness must enter our lives in order for us to become whole. Janet chose God's path.

Jeenie states, "My first inclination was fury toward Sister Modesta for damaging a precious young girl. An underdog can always be protected by me, if possible. I'll go to whatever limits I have at my disposal."

It's perfectly OK to be furious at injustice. Jesus was. Remember when He threw out the moneychangers and overturned their bird cages and tables because they were cheating the worshippers who came to the temple? The whip in Jesus's hand cleared out the abusers.

IN THE NEXT STORY, Shelia resolved never again to let her husband's addiction control her.

Singing the Victory
Shelia Leager

My husband used to intentionally stage a scene or argument with me for an excuse to leave our home. You see, if he could create an illusion of me being at fault, then he could say, "I wouldn't be going to the bar tonight if you hadn't been arguing with me." Now I realize that this is an old trick of an addict, but I fell for it for years. Alone in the house, I sat and cried, blaming myself for not keeping my mouth shut, while he sat at a bar, relishing his moments of glory.

Guess what? I finally woke up to his little plot. One evening he started in again. Nothing suited him—not dinner, not the house, not the kids—nothing. He knew exactly how to push my buttons.

That evening I started to react as I always had, but then it hit me. *No,* my mind screamed. *If he leaves to go to the bar, it's because he wants to be there. He'll have to accept responsibility for his actions because I'm not going to spend my evening in tears!* At that moment I decided I'd no longer be a puppet in his little theatrics. I would no longer accept that there was a flaw in my character that chased him off to a bar.

I smiled and began a little march around the house. As I stomped through the house toward him, I said, "You can be mean and nasty if you want to, but I am going to sing!" As I stomped in a circle around my kitchen, at the top of my voice and well out of tune, I bellowed out an old song, "Victory in Jesus." When I began singing, I felt angry, fed up, and on a mission. But the more I sang, the happier I got. The next thing I knew, I was honestly singing the song from my heart and didn't care if he left or not.

In the midst of the song, I heard a belly laugh coming from the living room. Believe it or not, my husband was laughing. He looked at me and said, "I wish I had your faith."

Four things happened in that moment:

1. If he wanted to leave, he would have to accept the fact that he was fooling no one.
2. I took away all his ammunition.
3. I gave myself permission to accept that it was not my fault.
4. I found out you can find joy in the darkest of circumstances.

"Good for Shelia! What a wonderful way to counteract the antics of a drunken, abusive husband!" Jeenie adds, "Not only did it lift her thoughts into heaven, but it brought to a halt the actions of her blaming, controlling husband."

In situations like this, rising above is imperative. Cowering in the corner does nothing but continue the victimization. That's how perpetrators work their evil deeds. Shelia figuratively took the emotional bullets from his gun. Shooting did no good anymore.

This is a healthy response and one which needs to be continually practiced in order to survive the onslaughts of a person who throws around damaging words and actions.

In the Book of Job we find that godly man's story preserved for all generations. It shows an interesting plea from a man whose grief caused him to wish he'd never been born. Even in the midst of his suffering, Job continued to praise God.

> "Oh, that my words were recorded, that they were written on a scroll, that they were inscribed with an iron tool on lead, or engraved in rock forever! I know that my redeemer lives."
> —Job 19:23–25

One of the highlights of Job's true story describes a day in heaven when the angels presented themselves before God. Even Satan joined them. God asked Satan a question: *"Have you considered my servant Job? There is no one on earth like him; he is blameless and upright, a man who fears God and shuns evil"* (Job 1:8).

Satan challenged God concerning Job, *"But stretch your hand out and strike everything he has, and he will surely curse you to your face"* (Job 1:11).

Job went about his normal routine unaware that Satan circled him like a bird of prey. Job enjoyed being a husband, father, and successful businessman. His life had been blessed with great wealth. Yet before long, hopelessness would vanquish hope, tears would drown laughter, and sorrow would steal joy. In a single day messengers brought news to Job of great disasters. All seven of Job's sons and three daughters were killed. His vast herds of sheep, oxen, and donkeys were stolen or destroyed. Finally, boils covered Job's entire body.

> *His wife said to him, "Are you still holding on to your integrity? Curse God and die!"*
>
> *He replied, "You are talking like a foolish woman. Shall we accept good from God, and not trouble?"*
>
> —Job 2:9–10

Job's friends, Eliphaz, Bildad, and Zophar, heard about Job's problems and with good intentions set out to sympathize and comfort him. They wept when they saw Job because the sores had ravaged him, making it difficult to recognize him.

They sat with Job for seven days and remained silent. But as they struggled to find an explanation for Job's situation, they began discussions and arguments about why catastrophe struck Job's life. In conclusion, they accused Job of sinning and decreed that sin was the reason for God's punishment. They implored Job to repent. At one point Job replied:

> *I have heard many things like these;*
> *   miserable comforters are you all!*
> *Will your long-winded speeches never end?*
> *What ails you that you keep on arguing?*
> *I also could speak like you,*
> *   if you were in my place;*
> *I could make fine speeches against you*
> *   and shake my head at you.*
> *But my mouth would encourage you;*
> *   comfort from my lips would bring you relief.*
> *   —Job 16:2–5*

Scripture discloses Job's heartwrenching struggle with God as Job expressed his need for understanding. God answered Job with such a profound series of questions that Job was humbled by God's sovereignty. He accepted the truth that God's ways are too great at times for understanding.

Then God spoke to Job's friends. He was not pleased with their self-righteous judgments against Job. They had been arguing among themselves instead of praying to God for understanding; they had belittled and condemned their friend, causing more pain.

We read God's response to Job's friends in Job 42:7: "*I am angry with you and your two friends, because you have not spoken of me what is right, as my servant Job has.*"

They must have trembled when they heard those words. We might wonder what they thought when God told them: "*My servant Job will pray for you, and I will accept his prayer and not deal with you according to your folly*" (Job 42:8).

Job forgave his friends for their unkind words, and God blessed Job's remaining years even more than he had before. The spiritual challenge between Satan and God not only changed Job's life and strengthened his faith but also is a reminder that there are times in our own lives when we must also stop and ask, "Shall we accept only good from God, and not trouble?"

Reflections

Describe positive reasons not to suffer in silence.

Lord, please take away my fear of rejection,
so that I no longer suffer in silence.

CHAPTER 6

Fork in the Road

I will lead the blind by ways they have not known,
*   along unfamiliar paths I will guide them;*
I will turn the darkness into light before them
*   and make the rough places smooth*
These are the things I will do;
*   I will not forsake them.*
                    —Isaiah 42:16

We have all turned on our computers to check email only to have an exasperating advertisement pop up. But then there are messages from friends: humorous ones that make us laugh, informative ones that help us stay close to one another, and inspirational ones that cause us to think about God. These are the messages that make the inconveniences of email worthwhile.

A daily email that brightens Karen's day arrives from her friend, Freda Fullerton, who is a senior citizen. Since Freda loves reaching out to people, she started an email ministry called Thought for the Day. One message really touched Karen's heart. It read: "God has a plan. He always does, but sometimes people forget and try to make their own imperfect plans. People can only see a little way down the road, but God can see the whole trip."

If life were always a straight path, we wouldn't be faced with decisions to make. However, often we encounter forks in the road, and at that moment we need to choose which way to go.

One of the meanings of the word *fork* is "division." Verbal abuse causes division. When emotional mistreatment has reached a point in our lives where we realize that we cannot cope anymore, we come to a crossroad. We know we must change the direction of our lives or give up. We are reminded that God is in control. When we are faced with a crisis, we know a choice is required. It isn't easy to change our thinking and move out of the box of victimization into the open space of God's love. We have been indoctrinated for so long, we ourselves believe we don't deserve better.

In Max Lucado's book *It's Not About Me* he states,

> With change comes fear, insecurity, sorrow, stress. So what do you do? Hibernate? Take no risks for fear of failing? Give no love for fear of losing? Some opt to hold back. . . . A better idea is to look up. Set your bearing on the one and only North Star in the universe—God. For though life changes, He never does.

As victims of abuse how do we withstand the acts of others? The abuse has to stop; we are sick of our lifestyle. Yet here we stand at a fork in the road—frozen, unable to take that first step. We've prayed. We've sat in church with smiles that feel like they've been pasted on our faces. Inside we are dying a little more each day. How then do we turn faith into action?

When we reach a moment of truth, we realize that we must take that first step toward changing our lives. Here are some tips on doing that:

- Remember the journey starts with you.
- Focus on the road ahead that will bring healing.
- Don't look back.
- Know that God is walking with you.

TONYA STOOD AT A FORK in the road after the death of her mother. She questioned, *Why do I remember all the bad memories? Why can't I remember the good times?* The following story shows how Tonya Ruiz took that first step.

Letting Go, One Word at a Time
Tonya Ruiz

Startled awake, I answered the phone and heard Dad's voice, "Your mom's in the emergency room. They think she's had a stroke."

On the drive to the hospital I felt sick to my stomach as I remembered my last phone conversation with Mom.

"Are you going to repaint your kitchen?" Mom had asked.

"I just painted it."

"It looks pink."

"Mom, its beige, and it matches my tiles."

"Did Ron finish building the pantry?"

"No, he hasn't had time."

"I couldn't live without a pantry."

"I guess it's a good thing you don't live here, isn't it, Mom? I've got to go."

My thoughts returned to the present, as I entered the hospital. Instead of rushing to Mom's side I detoured into the bathroom. Locking the stall door, I leaned against it and sobbed until I couldn't breathe. *Why does it have to be this way?* I asked God. *My mother is sick. I know I should go to her, but I can't—I just can't.*

God, please change my attitude and help me to forgive Mom for always being so critical and negative toward me. This may be the only chance to make peace with her. I can't do this on my own. Please help me.

Before I left the bathroom, I splashed cold water on my red, swollen face.

As I walked into the emergency room cubicle, I saw the

woman who had given birth to me. I grieved because of the wall of anger that separated us.

"Hello, Mom." Turning to the doctor I asked, "Have you run any tests yet?"

"Pssst." My mother motioned for me to come over.

"What, Mom?"

Pointing to her lunch tray, she whispered, "Someone has stolen the cherries out of my fruit cocktail."

The stroke had left Mom childlike, but after a few days, as the swelling in her brain subsided, her memory returned. She began to act like her old self.

"Isn't that the fattest nurse you've ever seen?"

"Shhh," I whispered.

"She can't hear me."

"She's overweight, Mom, not deaf."

"How can she do her job correctly?"

"Gosh, Mom. Would you stop?"

"Do I embarrass you?"

"Well," I said collecting my stuff, "I had better get going."

My mother had been a Christian from an early age, but the bitterness that permeated her life kept her from walking close to the Lord.

At home, I told my husband, "It's a miracle she's still alive. Yet she is so rebellious in her heart toward God. How can that be?"

Shortly after she was discharged from the hospital to recover at home, I had to leave town on a business trip. One ring of the hotel phone, and I knew something was wrong. Dad said, "Tonya, you need to come home. Your mom's back in the hospital, and it doesn't look good."

In intensive care, I saw my mother hooked up to monitors and IVs. An oxygen mask helped to ease her labored breathing. She reached for my hand and whispered, "I'm afraid. Please stay until I'm asleep."

Over the next few days, she introduced me to the nurses with, "Have you met my baby?"

Once when we were alone Mom asked, "Tonya, what are they going to do now?"

"I don't know, Mom. There's a specialist who might be able to help you."

"What if he can't fix me?"

"Then you get to go to heaven first and wait for the rest of us. Is that OK?

"Tonya, you can get so sick that you don't care to live anymore."

"Are you at peace about dying?"

She nodded her head. We cried together.

I brought her my CD player, and the sound of old hymns like "Beulah Land" and "I'd Rather Have Jesus" brought her comfort. Amazingly, every time I left the room, she kissed me and said, "I love you."

One morning when I arrived, she asked, "Guess who came to visit me?"

"I don't have any idea, Mom."

"Your pastor!"

"Really?"

Is she going to be mad at me? I wondered.

"Honestly, Mom, I didn't ask him to come."

"I know you didn't. He said he just decided to drop by."

"What happened? Did you throw your flowers at him?" I teased.

"It was really nice. We talked for a while, and then we prayed."

"Mom, that's wonderful."

"Praise the Lord," Mom whispered.

Finally, Mom was at peace with her Savior, but each day her physical condition worsened. I held her hand as a single tear rolled down her cheek. Then with her last breath, I became motherless.

At her funeral, I began remembering past wrongs and accusations, and I wore my hurts like an old tattered bathrobe.

Later, I called my lifelong friend Lisa and asked, "You knew my mother. Maybe I didn't try hard enough to get along with her."

"Tonya, your mother was an extremely difficult person. You tried."

Months later at home, I stood in the hall and stared at my family pictures hanging on the wall. "Why am I smiling in those pictures? I don't remember being happy as a child," I said to my husband, who took me into his arms.

"Sweetheart, your mom is gone. You need to move on with your life," he consoled.

When friends at church asked, "Do you miss your mom?" I didn't dare tell them, "No, I'm relieved she's not around trying to control my life." I felt guilty.

Over cappuccinos I asked my friend Nancy, "How do I put this all behind me? How do I forget all the hurtful things that she said to me?"

"Tonya, forgiveness is not as simple as erasing a blackboard. It's not a specific event, but more of a process. You let go word by word, syllable by syllable, and comma by comma. Time will help."

Mom's house sold. While going through her things and packing them away, I found an old black-and-white picture of my mother and myself as a blonde-headed toddler, cuddled together on the beach. As I stared at that faded photograph, I realized that Mom wasn't perfect, but she did love me.

That day I determined not to wallow in a past that I couldn't change. Forgiveness begins with a decision. I had to let go of the memories of my mother's demeaning comments. I had kept them and fed them like crows in a birdcage for too long. I decided to open the cage, and one by one, I set them free. Sometimes, I still hear them cawing outside my window, but I choose not to let them in.

● ● ●

Thankfully, Tonya's story of her mother ends with a redeeming quality. However, Jeenie states, "This is quite an unusual situation—one for which we all long, but one that seldom occurs. Most often, we are left with the stony silence of unspoken words of love, affirmation, or confession.

"Tonya determined to begin the journey of forgiveness, realizing it would set her free. My firm belief is that God has not suggested we forgive—He commanded it. He knows the freedom forgiveness brings, and in His divine and perfect love for us, His desire is that we experience the very best. Thus, forgiveness is a compassionate edict."

There are several stages to forgiveness:

- Stage one is admitting the pain. Don't excuse or make light of what the perpetrator has done.
- Stage two is dealing with the anger. Allow a healthy anger to emerge, but do not dwell on it. We need to give up our right for revenge and eventually move through the rage.
- Stage three is confronting the perpetrator, although most of us shy away from it. Sometimes confrontation may take place face-to-face; other times we may approach the person in a letter. A note needs to be short and to the point, letting the person know the damage we have experienced. It is vital to use "I" words, not "you" words. Saying, "You hurt me so deeply" is blaming. Instead, say, "I was hurt so deeply."

Forgive and forget—what a stupid statement! Rarely do we forget an injustice that has caused enormous pain. Granted, some of the details may become foggy, but we do remember.

When we forgive, even though our minds may not forget the injustice, we give up the right to retaliate—not easily done, but imperative. We do not seek revenge.

As we plod along the road toward wholeness in our forgiveness journey, a day will come when the event is no longer significant. Even though our memory is not totally eradicated, the situation no longer encompasses the totality of our life.

One word of caution: Tiny residual feelings remain—anger, hurt, and related emotions. However, these feelings will be fleeting, momentary segments. We can handle the moments, because that person no longer has a stranglehold on our life.

Jeenie concludes that traveling the path to forgiveness is hard, but the rewards are eternal.

IN THE FOLLOWING STORY Pat learned to overcome the stigma of "stupid," which was placed on her by her mother.

"Not So!"
Pat Johnson

Didn't my parents realize that their fears were going to affect my entire life?

Maybe they didn't stop to think that children overhear the things adults say. Typically when they talked to one another or to a friend or relative, I'd repeatedly hear comments like: "You say she might have been brain damaged at birth? You certainly wouldn't know it. She seems fine to me."

My mother always answered the same way, "Well, we don't know for sure, but after being born breach and not breathing, it's certainly possible."

Hearing the term *brain damaged* in reference to me left a scar on my heart. Doubt filled my mind and damaged my self-esteem. All through school anytime a problem arose, I'd hear that term again.

I was told over and over again, "Can't you do anything right?"

So by the time I reached fifth grade, I began to believe the old tapes that played in my mind. *I guess it's true,* I thought. *I must have been brain damaged. Does that mean I'm stupid?*

That word *stupid* stabbed me from then on whenever I did something wrong. I never openly talked with my parents about my pain and doubt, or how defeated my self-image had become. No, instead my silent wound festered deeply, quietly keeping me from reaching God's potential in my life.

In junior high and later in high school, I didn't even try to prepare for college. Instead, I majored in art. Subconsciously I chose classes I knew I would not fail.

I married right out of high school and spent the next four decades raising a family. My life felt secure and protected until the unthinkable happened—my husband died. Widowed at the age of 50, I still had a 14-year-old daughter to raise. We received Social Security until she turned 18 and left home. Then I needed to go to work, though I had zero experience or self-confidence.

Terrified, I began preparing myself for the working world. "I'll be happy to help out in the church office," I volunteered. Although I felt safe there, my typing skills left a lot to be desired. At the end of each day I told myself, *It's time for me to go back to school.*

I registered at a vocational school in a medical assistant's course. One year later, I graduated and went to work in a doctor's office. The office manager and I got along well. She trained me and treated me kindly, and my confidence increased.

Then five months later the manager said, "Pat, I'm sorry, but I have to let you go. The doctor is offended that you don't understand what he says. He said no one else has trouble with his accent. Yesterday, when you asked him to repeat his orders in front of Mrs. James, she later complained that this made her feel unsafe."

I turned to God for help. I prayed, "Lord, I feel so stupid. I've failed again." Then another thought entered my mind, "Over the years I've learned that other people make mistakes, too. I'm not alone. I'm human. Isn't that what You're trying to tell me, Lord?"

From that moment on every time the word *stupid* tried to stab me, I replied, "*Not so.*" I wouldn't accept it as the truth about me. I recalled a Scripture verse I had learned. *"For who has known the mind of the Lord that he may instruct him? But we have the mind of Christ"* (1 Corinthians 2:16).

The Lord blessed me with the perfect job when my son said, "Mom, I need help with my computer business. I want you to come work for me." There I worked until I retired, loving every minute of my job.

Now as a senior citizen, I face moments of memory loss. From time to time I find myself saying, *"You're stupid."* But once again I gently remind myself, *"Not so!"*

● ● ●

Children learn to stuff their feelings, living a life of pretense. Often, even with their closest friends, they do not risk being vulnerable. Pat's fear of being stupid created a sense of shame that kept her from sharing her feelings with her best friends. She was afraid they thought she was stupid, too, so she always hid—hoping it was not true. She truly believed the messages her mother drilled into her mind and heart, and she acted accordingly until she turned to God for help.

Most stories do not turn out as well as Pat's. People remain stuck, unable to surmount the wounding that has occurred. Jeenie's office is full of adults who continue to flounder because they live their lives based on the negative, untrue, and hurting comments, made especially in childhood, by someone they loved and trusted.

When we are wounded by words, they stick—forever. Even if we have excelled in life, the memory does not leave. Although the scar will always be there, when hope and healing occur, the ugly wound will no longer fester.

Wounded by Words

Hidden

Connie L. Peters

They like me.
They laugh at my jokes.
They seek my advice.
They enjoy my creativity.
They desire my company.
They put their hands in mine, and we walk together.

They need my help.
They need my clever ideas.
They miss me when I'm absent.
They seek me out.
They pray for me.
They passionately care for me.
But all this is only in my imagination.

From their point of view:
She is plain.
She is shy.
She has no personality.
She looks at her toes.
She frowns.
We have to walk on eggshells around her.
We dare not tease; she may cry.
We may pray for her once in a while—when we think of it.

Perhaps someday she'll come out of her shell.
But most of the time,
Like a wall,
We never see her at all.

They don't see
The person I call me.

Pearl Bailey once stated, "You never find yourself until you face the truth." Are you ready to face the reasons behind your pain? We must be willing to let go of the issues that keep us trapped within the jaws of verbal abuse.

HOW DOES AN ADULT CHILD deal with continual verbal abuse from a parent? Many women have grown up with a parent whose ill-treatment tore down their self-esteem. Some adult children completely walk away from their parent, making the decision to end a hurtful relationship. Then there are others who choose to love and forgive. Susan demonstrates this truth in the following story.

The $2,000 Weekend from Hell
Susan Titus Osborn

As I drove up Pacific Coast Highway toward Santa Barbara, my stomach churned. *I should be looking forward to a relaxing summer getaway at the beautiful Biltmore Hotel located right on the beach—but I feel only dread.*

Over the years, there had been vacations with Mother that brought happy memories of flying kites, searching for shells, and watching my two sons on their boogie boards. Occasionally, she'd been verbally abusive, yet somehow we still had fun.

Then Mother suffered a mild stroke in 1990 on the day after Christmas. For the most part, she seemed to recover, but her personality changed drastically. She began drinking heavily, and when she drank, she became extremely verbally abusive.

I hadn't seen Mother in months, so I felt apprehensive. How would Mother greet me? I pulled into the parking lot. Once inside I registered at the desk. Just as I reached our room, a bell cap breezed past me and said over his shoulder, "We tried three rooms before we found one to your mother's liking. I just fixed her a drink. Now you're all set."

Sure, we're all set, Mother's already drinking, and I can hardly wait to hear her negative comments.

I thanked the young man and closed the door behind me. Mother sat in a chair, drink in hand, and looked up with bloodshot eyes. Obviously, she'd had more than one cocktail.

"Hello, Mother, how are you?" The knot in my stomach tightened.

"I thought they would never find me a suitable room. I told them over the phone the exact room I wanted. But they made me traipse all over the hotel grounds. Don't they know I have trouble walking? No consideration, especially, after my long, horrific flight."

At dinner, she continued drinking and ranted and raved about the service. Then she looked at me. "Where'd you get that outfit? It looks terrible. And your hair—why don't you let it grow long again? Why haven't you lost any weight since the last time I saw you?"

I didn't defend myself or my attire. Instead I said, "Mother, let me help you back to the room." She stumbled as she tried to get out of her chair. I took her arm so she wouldn't fall flat on her face.

Back in our luxurious suite, she screamed, "You're selfish. You only think of yourself. Your grandparents spoiled you. Now no one can do anything with you."

On and on her monologue went, until I reached a point where I couldn't take anymore. At 47, I felt like a helpless child again. I put on my swimsuit and calmly said, "Mother, I'm going to relax in the Jacuzzi. I'll see you later."

"Don't you leave me! I'm not through talking to you! Come back here!"

I kept walking. I had to get away for a while. I stayed in the Jacuzzi for almost an hour. Returning to our room I found Mother asleep, lying sideways across her bed, with her clothes still on. I covered her and slipped into my own bed.

At lunch the next day Mother ordered a drink.

Oh no. Here we go again.

Mother had grown up in a wealthy family, with her own African American nanny to take care of her every wish and whim. But when she married my dad and moved in with his folks, she learned about middle class. Grandma Ruthie expected everyone in the house to chip in and help with the housecleaning.

During lunch Mother said, "Ruthie made me clean the toilets. Can you imagine—me cleaning toilets!"

No, I couldn't imagine what a shock that had been for my mother. She had never been prepared for the real world. She felt resentful toward her mother-in-law—resentment that, sadly, lasted her whole life.

As Mother talked about the past I realized how her views on life were far from what I considered to be the norm. Money was Mother's security, but it hadn't brought her happiness. After my stepfather died, she had wealth but an empty heart.

As I sat in that lovely restaurant overlooking the water, I stared at my mother. *Thank You, Lord, for the gift of insight and understanding about Mother.*

● ● ●

"Susan showed God-honoring kindness and wisdom as she dealt with her drunken mother," Jeenie states. "Susan didn't try to defend herself against her mother's accusations in her inebriated state. It never works. It's like talking to a wall. Instead, Susan removed herself from the situation, graciously but firmly."

In any abusive situation, it is best to state you are leaving—then go. The key is to be firm and gentle—soft in the delivery of the message, but unyielding in the stance.

Jeenie's elderly father (now deceased) was thrown out of three convalescent homes because he was mean to the residents and caregivers. A man filled with anger, he perpetrated emotional and physical abuse in his family. He left their home when Jeenie was a child.

Viewing childhood photos of her father caused Jeenie's heart to go out to him and helped her to understand him—and eventually to forgive. He once said that his father had continually told him he was illegitimate, even though he looked like his eight brothers.

As Jeenie looked at his innocent face as a four-year-old, she began to realize how deeply he had been hurt by a father whom he loved and needed. Anger eventually welled up in her father, and he, in turn, became an abuser.

Viewing pictures of our parents as children and understanding their upbringing is a good way to get a handle on the abuse that is passed down to us.

Have you ever been insulted by someone you went to for help? Did anger burn like a blazing sun, causing a thirst for revenge? We read in 1 Samuel 25 of such an incident where David and his men took refuge in the desert region of Maon. Campfires burned into the night. The 600 men went about various duties, tending horses, setting up sleep areas, and discussing plans for the next day. David had shown kindness to the nearby shepherds by circling their herds with his men. Robbers wouldn't dare go near.

Sheep shearing was a festive event, and David sent ten of his men to request provisions from the wealthy owner, Nabal. Surely Nabal would repay their kindness with kindness.

But the friendly greetings from David's men were ignored. Surly and crude in his dealings with others, Nabal hurled insults at David's men:

*"Who is this David? "Who is this son of Jesse? Many
servants are breaking away from their masters these days.
Why should I take my bread and water, and the meat
I have slaughtered for my shearers, and give it to men
coming from who knows where?"*
                                         —1 Samuel 25:10–11

Beads of sweat beat across the brows of David's
messengers as they hurried back to camp to report word for
word what Nabal had said.

When David received their report his heart began to race and
his facial muscles tightened with determination. Anger blew like
a hot surging desert wind and turned his mind toward revenge.

"Put on your swords," he shouted. The ground shook
under the weight of David's army of 400 men as they rode
toward Nabal's home.

Meanwhile in Nabal's household, a servant rushed to find
Nabal's wife, Abigail. The servant had witnessed the events
between his master and David's men. He needed to warn
Abigail of the impending danger. Beautiful and kind, Abigail
also had a reputation for her wisdom.

Who would better know the truth regarding Nabal than
his wife? She listened intently and did not dispute the servant's final statement about Nabal: "He is such a wicked man
that no one can talk to him."

Abigail worked quickly to put together provisions for
David and his men. Meanwhile, the story continues:

*David had just said, "It's been useless—all my watch-
ing over this fellow's property in the desert so that
nothing of his was missing. He has paid me back evil
for good. May God deal with David, be it ever so
severely, if by morning I leave alive one male of all
who belong to him!"*
                                         —1 Samuel 25:21–22

David saw a woman just ahead, riding her donkey up the mountain ravine. When Abigail reached him, she climbed down from her donkey and bowed before David:

She fell at his feet and said: "My Lord, let the blame be on me alone. Please let your servant speak to you; hear what your servant has to say. May my lord pay no attention to that wicked man Nabal. He is just like his name— his name is Fool, and folly goes with him. But as for me, your servant, I did not see the men my master sent."
—1 Samuel 25:24 25

Abigail showed respect for David. The provisions she brought were proof of her sincerity, and she gave God the glory. Abigail gently revealed six vital truths God placed on her heart to share with David:
- The Lord keeps you from bloodshed.
- The Lord keeps you from revenge.
- Forgive your servant's offense.
- The Lord will deal with your enemies.
- The Lord will keep His promises to you.
- The Lord has brought you success.

David listened and accepted what Abigail shared. His final words to her were, "*Go home in peace. I have heard your words and granted your request*" (1 Samuel 24:35).

Abigail returned home to boisterous voices, free-flowing wine, and a drunken husband strutting around his banquet like a king. Wisely, she decided to wait until morning before sharing with Nabal. As Abigail described all of the events surrounding the near disaster, Nabal suffered a heart attack. Ten days later he died.

When the news reached David, he praised God for upholding his cause. Soon thereafter Abigail became David's wife.

A gentle answer turns away wrath, but a harsh word stirs up anger.

—Proverbs 15:1

Reflections

What keeps you trapped in a lifestyle of abuse?

Lord, I am unsure how to proceed. I know I don't want to continue in a life of abuse.

CHAPTER 7

Becoming Real

I know your deeds. See, I have placed before you
an open door that no one can shut.
I know that you have little strength,
yet you have kept my word and have not denied my name.
—Revelation 3:8

So much of our conversation with other people is on a surface level. If we see friends at church or out shopping, they will probably ask, "How are you?" Ninety-nine percent of the time, we will reply, "I'm fine. How are you?" Yet, so often, we aren't fine. We paste a smile on our faces and pretend that all is well when we are actually hurting inside.

Susan went on a women's church retreat where the participants gathered in groups of three or four. They were asked to share their greatest concerns with the other members of their small group. They all promised that anything said in the group stayed in the group and would not be repeated elsewhere. This created an environment for the women to open their hearts, make themselves vulnerable, and share what was really on their minds. They became real.

Often those who are verbally abused build huge walls around their hearts to protect themselves from further abuse. They paste on a smiley face, avoid subjects that will anger their abuser, and go about their lives as if they didn't have a care in the world. Yet they live in fear that they will say or do something to aggravate their husband, parent, or whoever is abusing them. As a result they lose a little of themselves in the process, and they may reach a point where they don't know who they really are or what is really important to them.

As a child, Debbie suffered verbal abuse from her father. She carried feelings of insecurity into her marriage, which made it easy for her husband to manipulate her and make her feel overweight and frumpy when that wasn't the case at all.

One Size Fits All
Debbie Thompson

Although I grew up in a Christian family who stressed the inner values of godliness, character, honesty, and love, I always found myself seeking my father's affirmation. As a child, my father repeatedly told me, "On the day you were born, I passed out cigars and told my co-workers I had twin boys." His face revealed a smile as if he were telling a joke; however, his eyes told a different story—one of disappointment. I was a girl who liked dolls, and although I also liked horses, the outdoors, and athletics, I was not the tomboy my father tried to make me into.

Then at 24, I married Robert, a man who appreciated my feminine qualities. What I never realized at the time, though, was that he wanted a Barbie doll. Although beauty queen crowns and cheerleading uniforms hung in my closet, they didn't change my name to Barbie, nor my shape to hers.

For years, Robert subjected me to verbal and nonverbal abuse every time I wanted to taste a dessert. He'd say, "You don't need that. That is what undisciplined fat people eat."

I would respond, "This is what normal people eat."

Over the years I began to believe that I was fat and undisciplined. I grew weary of the arguments and my husband's sulking, and I stopped defending myself. After we had children, my husband purchased many of my clothes. He chose beautiful, revealing clothes that displayed the sculpted trophy of my husband's dreams. He insisted that I always wear makeup, and he'd grab my stomach and say, "Checking those love handles."

I became a full-time mother to our two children and gained ten pounds. I then wore a size 6, to which Robert said, "You are falling into this pudgy mother thing." That Christmas he gave me a gym membership, workout clothes, and a personal trainer.

Constantly, I heard him say, "Did you go to the gym today?" Other phrases included, "Are you really going to eat all of that?" and "Let me check out your abs this week."

I competed in every possible athletic endeavor and won lots of trophies. At age 42, I continued winning figure and natural bodybuilding contests. Yet, I felt worn out and empty emotionally. I became depressed about my personal life. My energies were always focused on my children, my husband, and others. My physical health started to suffer. I remained the perfect trophy on the outside with a sad worn-out soul on the inside.

I sought a Christian counselor who helped me set boundaries and establish priorities. I thought a perfect home consisted of June and Ward Cleaver from the TV show *Leave It to Beaver*. My counselor pointed out the mutual respect shown in that show and what the Bible states about marriage and a godly home. I realized that changes in my marriage were necessary. I also understood that we can train people how to treat us by setting healthy boundaries.

From that point on, when the jabs came, I repeated many canned phrases such as, "Does it make you a man to verbally abuse your wife?" Not only did I stand up to Robert, but I would tell the children, "Respect and love make a happy home." When Robert started to sulk, I would ignore him for days until he apologized. I also asked him to repeat ten compliments for every insult.

We both needed to change. My husband's desire for a Barbie and his obsession for perfection were not my problem. I needed to stop enabling the bad behavior and focus on God's plan for me.

I told Robert, "The only way our marriage can continue is if you seek counseling for your insecurities."

In therapy he faced voices from his past and found the courage to overcome some generational issues. Our communication improved greatly as he began to respect me and grew in understanding.

Meanwhile I gained 20 pounds of happiness. I rediscovered the passions of my childhood. Today I eat chocolate guilt free and take care of myself. There is such a freedom when you step out in faith and start becoming who the Lord created you to be.

Our marriage is wonderful, and we are growing as individuals and as a couple. I have started a freelance writing career. I hit the gym three times a week, wear a size 6, and haven't seen my six-pack abs in months.

The voice that rings in my head today tells me that I'm created in God's image. Nowhere in the Bible do I find verses that state we have to be a certain physical size to serve Him. I know that I am the daughter of the King, and I have accepted God's freedom and affirmation.

I have traded in the steps of a treadmill for steps on the path the Lord has laid out for my life. I love my new threads! The message on the tag states, "One size fits all."

● ● ●

"If you will notice," Jeenie says, "the changes came when Debbie began to face the reality of her situation. In the past, with both father and husband, she operated out of fear—fear of displeasing them and not measuring up to the standards they continually set. The harder Debbie reached for approval, the higher their expectations became."

One interesting comment is that Debbie swung the pendulum from passive to aggressive—moving from giving in and being a pleaser, to taking control of her actions toward her husband. In the instances where he sulked, she ignored his silent treatment for days until he apologized. She asked that he give ten compliments for every insult, and she encouraged him to go to therapy. That's taking control, but it may not work in every situation.

To Debbie's credit, she no longer cringes from her husband's comments. Instead, she sought therapy, went to the gym, and is back in a size 6—for herself. She has learned to be an emotionally and spiritually healthy woman.

IN THE FOLLOWING STORY, Valerie was not so fortunate. She struggled with shame and hid from the truth.

Passing the Test
Wanda J. Burnside

At our fall teachers meeting, the new kindergarten teacher stood at the door, extending her hand to us. "Hi, I'm Valerie Hopkins," she said with a warm smile. Our school needed a motivated kindergarten teacher, and she came with high recommendations.

Our principal, Reverend Brown, said, "I like her attitude. She's what we need."

Following the meeting, she picked up her stack of books and swung her gigantic tote bag over her tiny shoulder.

"Let me help you," I suggested as we walked together.

She smiled. "You're Mrs. Burnside."

"Yes, I'm the first- and second-grade teacher. My room is across from yours."

She handed me her books. "Hi, neighbor," she said. "Thanks."

We walked to her classroom. She had decorated it with colorful charts and cutouts.

"Wow. It looks wonderful. When did you…"

"I came to town early to set up the apartment I'm renting," she said. "My husband works out of town, so he can't help me."

That afternoon we went to lunch and in time became close friends. She worked hard with her students. I could hear her singing, laughing, counting, and reading stories to them.

As Thanksgiving approached I asked, "Valerie, what are you and your husband doing for the holiday?"

"I'm going to finish unpacking. We're staying at home."

"You're welcome to join us." On Thanksgiving I called her and became concerned when the operator said her phone wasn't in service. So, my husband, Simmie, and I drove over to her house.

A car I didn't recognize sat in her driveway. I stepped out of our car and walked up to her porch. I could hear shouting from inside. Valerie screamed, "No! Get away from me!"

When I heard glass breaking, I jumped off the porch and ran back to the safety of my own car. Just then, a chair flew through the window. Valerie ran out, and Simmie opened our car door and let her in.

"Go! Take me away from here!" she cried. "I'm so sorry."

"We're taking you to the police station," Simmie said. "Who was that? What's going on?"

"That's a friend. I mean, he's someone from my past." After a pause, Valerie cried, "Please don't take me to the police. I can't explain this situation." Then after another pause, she exclaimed, "Take me back!"

"Don't go back!" I pleaded.

"You don't understand. . . .You need to take me home! He didn't mean it. I made him mad. I need to go back and set things right."

"Are you sure?" I asked. "What did you do to make him mad?"

"I said dumb things."

When we drove her home, the car was gone. We gave her the Thanksgiving box of food I had fixed for her. Valerie got out of our car and went in her apartment.

In the following weeks, I never mentioned what had happened, and Valerie didn't either.

Valerie seems happy, I thought.

But around Christmas, Valerie complained of headaches and stomach pain. She wore sunglasses to work.

I felt concerned and asked, "Why are your lips and eyes swollen?"

"Don't worry about it," she said, with an edge to her voice.

At Easter, we met her husband and went out to dinner together. During the summer they visited our church a few times. I felt hopeful.

But then in the fall, Valerie withdrew. She stopped dressing professionally and didn't decorate her classroom like the previous year. Her personality changed. She snapped at me, the children, and everyone else. Suddenly she didn't have a car anymore. We drove her home every day.

Then one day after school, Valerie stood in the doorway of my classroom and said, "Wanda, I've had enough of the lies. Brent didn't used to be hateful, but he is abusing me. My husband hates me because I have a job and a college degree. He calls me a dumb, stupid nobody. For years, he's hurt me and even threatened to kill me."

She paused, regaining her composure. "He's taken almost everything out of our apartment. The only possession I have is my Bible. I don't know who I am anymore. I've got to get help. I can't live like this anymore."

I walked over to Valerie and put my arms around her. I knew she was finally ready to face her situation, and Simmie and I would stand beside her every step of the way.

● ● ●

Literally scores of times Jeenie has heard similar stories in her therapy office. The victim will excuse the physical and verbal abuse as did Valerie: "I said dumb things." Constant pretending and hiding the scars is par for the course. Always the victim thinks, *It will get better if I just do what I need to do and stop making him mad. It's all my fault.*

The perpetrator is highly manipulative; therefore, the victim returns again and again. "I'm so sorry and ashamed of the way I treated you," the perpetrator oozes, while touching a damaged face or body. "I promise to never hurt you again. Please don't leave me. My life is nothing without you." And on and on and on. Believing him, the wife readily forgives, and the new honeymoon period lasts about two weeks. Then, physical and/or emotional abuse again rears its ugly head.

Admitting the abuse is always the first step in getting help. There are shelters for women and their children—places of protection and counseling. Thousands of women survive physical abuse and become emotionally healthy after intense therapy.

ABIGAIL ALSO SOUGHT HELP to overcome the verbal abuse of her mother. At a turning point, Abigail asked, "How many times has my life been controlled by Mom's caustic words?"

Hatred Unveiled
Abigail Paul

I clenched the phone, sending silent pleas to God for help. I had no idea how to respond. My mother had barely left my home and was on the phone, telling me she planned to come back in a couple of weeks. I wasn't ready for the stress of her presence again so soon, but I had a hard time telling her so.

Oh, God! Show me what to say.

She droned on and on, discussing the details. I swallowed hard. "I don't think that will work with my schedule, Mom."

She prodded and pushed and cajoled. I stayed firm. "It's not a good time, Mom. You were just here, and it won't work for you to visit again so soon."

Then it started—the barrage of words I'd feared: ". . . selfish . . . have time for everyone but me . . . not the daughter I raised you to be . . . how can you deny me . . . uncaring . . ."

Her condemnation poured over the phone like a jammed CD, saying the same old stuff, shredding my nerves. I imagined a dagger, stabbing my heart again and again. Each time another slam rolled off Mom's tongue, my heart bled more. Each phrase killed another piece of me. Dead. Numb. I tried not to feel anything as she raged at me.

My teeth chattered. My body trembled as I fought for control, but something uncontrollable boiled inside me. "I hate you!" I hissed. Shocked, I hung up on her. *Oh, God, please! Please don't let me have said that loud enough for her to hear!*

Tears poured down my cheeks, and I rushed outside, seeking privacy. Huddled in a ball on the front steps, I sobbed. My husband came after me to see what was wrong. With quivering lips, I stuttered and stammered the story of what I'd done. What bothered me most was that I realized the angry words I'd spoken were true.

I hated my mother.

"How can a heart that is supposed to have Jesus inside experience such hate?" I asked. Unveiled, my true feelings mocked me, dark and menacing. My husband held me as I shook and cried. For years, I'd shoved down the effects of Mom's controlling, manipulative, hurtful words. I'd taken the blame, lived in guilt, and told myself I forgave her, as a good daughter should.

Now I knew differently. And I knew Jesus's love and my hatred should not cohabitate. The vehemence of my feelings petrified me. I faced the fact that I was not OK. The churning inside me was not something I could handle on my own. It wasn't going away. That night was the turning point.

The next week I sought help and began a process of admitting the abuse I'd suffered because of my mother, and I grieved it. Memories I'd shoved down deep now burst forth in unexpected moments, and tears often caught me unaware. I began to face all I'd endured, and as I did, I saw how my self-concept was shaped by the lies I'd believed in those moments. Most importantly, I learned that true forgiveness could come only when I was honest about my pain. Instead of making excuses for my mother and shoving down the agonizing emotions, I faced the abuse, grieved it, and then chose true forgiveness. I learned that forgiveness is a process. When other memories surfaced or fresh hurts came, I became angry, cried, and forgave again. And the hatred melted away.

New inner strength replaced the knotted, confused emotions I'd lived with for most of my life, and I found the courage to begin to draw boundaries with Mom. Over time, the churning inside became quiet. Now I live mostly in peace. There's a place in my heart that will always be sad and long for a healthy relationship with my mother, but I am no longer controlled by that need.

● ● ●

"Abigail's initial response was not unique," says Jeenie. "In fact it is quite common—the bleeding heart, numbness, and deep-seated anger that emerged into hatred. Whenever we do not confront our perpetrator, this is often the outcome."

Here is a way Abigail could have dealt with her mother in a more substantial, assertive way. When her mother started the degrading barrage, "You're selfish, uncaring, have time for everyone else," and so on, Abigail could have acknowledged her mother's feelings and responded to them.

She might have said, "Mom, I'm sure you are hurt that you will not be able to visit us again so soon. You feel like I do not love you or care about you, but I do love you. As I stated before, this will not be a good time for us. I'll talk to you again soon. I love you. Good-bye," and click down the telephone, without waiting for any response.

Using this technique, the one who is abused takes control of the conversation and ends it. If Mom interrupts, continue talking with no response to her, then say good-bye and hang up.

"One additional concept is how to deal with a mother-in-law," Jeenie adds. "It is not the same as dealing with your biological mother."

The advice Jeenie offers is to make your mother-in-law your friend, to whatever degree she will accept. Invite her to lunch. Brag about her son (your husband) and grandchildren, if there are any. Tell her the things you appreciate about her—you may need to think a bit on this one.

"Never, and I strongly suggest never, get into a confrontation or argument with her," continues Jeenie. "If there are issues, tell your husband and ask him to deal with his mother in whatever way he chooses.

"Blood runs deep. Your husband can say things that his mother will accept. Most of the time, it will be deadly if you go there. So stay away from it. If your husband chooses not to confront his mother, however, let it rest. Never cross the bloodline."

A Kind Word
Charles R. Brown

In our
grumbling,
fumbling,
stumbling
world,
there's someone
you can bless today.

But there is a cost.
It will involve several seconds
from that awful schedule
that demands your daily attention.

Three little words
may be enough to start with:
"I appreciate you."
Then tell them why.

None of us will ever grow
too old to be appreciated.

A word aptly spoken is like apples of gold in settings of silver.
—Proverbs 25:11

ALICIA WOULD EXPERIENCE the truth of this Scripture when she spoke the words, "God, please change me." God refined her like silver, taking out the impurities.

Memories
Alicia Goodwin

I was sweetly surprised by the phone call I received from my dad and his wife, Helen, calling from the southern state where I had grown up.

"Helen and I are going to be in San Diego next week," Dad said. "Maybe we can meet with you and Jason."

"Sure, it'll be great seeing y'all," I replied.

Placing the phone on the receiver, I thought, *I never dared to dream that someday my dad would be back into my life. As a little girl my mom's anger and verbal abuse convinced me he didn't want me anymore. How my heart ached for him when I was locked out in the backyard. I sat on my swing and pumped higher and higher, hoping God would see me, hear me, and make me feel good again. If I hadn't been run over by that truck ten years ago, I probably wouldn't even be talking to Dad. Sitting on my couch, I enveloped myself in memories—*

Threatening clouds loomed in the sky as I rode my bike on the way to the gym. Then a door to a parked car unexpectedly opened. Instinctively I swerved, realizing too late that my defensive maneuver placed me in oncoming traffic. A pickup truck struck me head-on.

The next thing I knew, I awoke in the hospital. A nurse called my brother, who was a paramedic, and said, "Alicia has been seriously injured. She has tire tracks going across her chest."

He replied, "I'll contact my dad, mom, brother, and sister. They're scattered all over the country, but I'll make sure they all come."

Suddenly, my chest felt heavy, and I went into full cardiac arrest. Emergency surgery was performed to save my life. When my family arrived, the surgeon said, "Although we didn't think Alicia would make it through surgery, we had to operate. Otherwise she would have no chance of survival."

Several days later, while heavily medicated, I awoke to see my entire family surrounding my bed. Tears ran down my face. Since I was connected to a ventilator, I couldn't speak. The last time I had visited with my dad was when I was six years old. Yet here he stood, looking down at me with concern in his eyes.

This must be bad if Dad's here.

I wanted to tell them how I'd poured out my heart to God the night before my accident. I prayed, "God, please change me. I've tried to leave behind my party lifestyle, but passing a joint with friends makes me feel accepted. Please heal my family and me."

Here I lay at 23 with numerous broken bones and a torn valve in my heart. I wondered, *Why me?*

A gentle voice whispered, *This will work together for good.*

How, God? I questioned.

Six months later, I walked out of that hospital smiling. All ten of my toes had been amputated, and I had a pig's valve in my heart. The multiple scars on my body portrayed a battle. Yet, I felt victorious in the renewed relationship with my family. But my greatest pleasure was knowing Dad truly cared. He even asked, "Alicia, would you like to come live with Helen and me?"

"Thanks, Dad, I'm flattered, but I need to stay in California. I plan to attend college."

My physical healing remained slow but steady. The first Sunday I could attend church I listened to our pastor read from Romans 8:28: *"And we know that in all things God works for the good of those who love him, who have been called according to his purpose."*

Wow! God told me it would work together for good, I marveled. The accident had drawn us together. What the enemy had tried to use for evil, God used for good.

But God wasn't finished with me yet. He began to bring my pain about Mom's verbal abuse to the surface. The reasons for her anger became real to me: At the age of three my mom, her five-year-old sister, and her mom fled Germany on foot. During World War II, her father died as a prisoner of war. At a young age Mom was sent to a strict boarding school. Years later Mom and Dad met and fell in love. He was in the army, stationed in Germany. When my parents married, my grandma disowned Mom. Years later, when Dad seemingly discarded her, too, by divorcing her, she endlessly labored to support her children, but she felt lonely and frustrated.

God's love helped me to forgive Mom for those years of lies and abuse. Through the horror of my accident, Mom showed me her love by being there for me. God allowed my resentment and hurt to slowly melt away. I began to feel compassion for her, which she accepted gratefully.

My heavenly Father became real to me in a very personal way. Truly He had healed my physical heart and pieced together my emotionally broken heart too.

I smiled as the memories faded—

When Dad and Helen arrived the next week, we had a great visit with each other. They treated Jason and me to a day at San Diego's Sea World. Upon departure, Dad hugged me and said, "I'm glad to see you so happy."

Thank You, God!

● ● ●

"During a dark time in my life," Jeenie says, "I asked God to help me understand Romans 8:28. He brought to me the illustration of baking a cake from scratch."

Picture the following:

- Select a large bowl, wooden spoon, measuring cup, and recipe. The first ingredient is a cup of shortening. Now, if you took a big spoonful and popped it into your mouth, you would spit it out.
- Next, comes two cups of sugar. Dumping it in your mouth would be far too much.
- Then add the raw eggs—hardly a taste treat.
- Then add three cups of flour. Even a tablespoon in your mouth would stick.
- Next comes baking soda, salt, and baking powder—repugnant stuff.
- Finally, add the chocolate. To your surprise, it's bitter. Yuk!

Each of these ingredients by itself is distasteful. However, when they are blended together, beaten, and baked in a hot oven, they become a mouth-watering treat.

So many things that happen to us are offensive, but God slowly and deliberately blends them together for our good. As we allow Him to work in our lives, He will turn disasters into blessings.

Luke 10:31–41 tells the story of two sisters, Mary and Martha. It is an account of everyday events during which Jesus helped Martha understand what is really important in life.

What's wrong with Mary? She knows food must be prepared. I told her that I'd invited Jesus and His disciples to eat with us. Martha felt resentment growing inside. Like a carpenter's clamp, it squeezed tightly around her mind and heart. Her chest heaved with anger, and her cheeks turned bright red. Martha had reached her limit. *Why is Mary sitting at the feet of Jesus and not helping me? Doesn't anyone care about how hard I'm working?*

She glanced once more into the room where everyone sat around Jesus, hoping to catch Mary's attention. But no, her sister was focused on Jesus's every word, oblivious to Martha's needs for help. Overwhelmed with anger, Martha stepped away from her food preparations to confront the matter.

Give yourself permission to visualize the next scene. Perhaps Jesus stopped talking and looked up at Martha as she entered the room. Maybe He listened to her with a compassionate smile.

"Lord, don't you care that my sister has left me to do the work by myself? Tell her to help me."

"Martha, Martha," the Lord answered, *"You are worried and upset about many things, but only one thing is needed. Mary has chosen what is better, and it will not be taken away from her."*
—Luke 10:40–41

Notice that Jesus did not scold Martha, but spoke truthfully and gently to her—as a father would to a child. He offered insight on her worrisome attitude, one that robbed her of happiness. He also told Martha that He would not take away from Mary the joy her decision had brought her.

Personalities often take a role in personal reactions and choices. No one asked Martha to prepare food. Martha made a personal choice to serve; after all, she was a hands-on, take-action type of woman. She concentrated on the physical needs of providing nourishment to everyone, and it became her main focus.

We've all experienced those times when worry clouds our perspective. Anger sneaks in the back door of our minds, and consequently we make accusations we really don't mean.

Temporarily Martha forgot the reason behind her service. Had Martha forgotten the miracles Jesus had already performed to feed the multitudes? In Mark 8:2–3, we read how He fed 4,000 with seven loaves of bread and a few fish:

"I have compassion for these people; they have already been with me three days and have nothing to eat. If I send them home hungry, they will collapse on the way, because some of them have come a long distance."

If Martha had chosen to sit at the feet of Jesus next to Mary, would Jesus not have met all their needs?

Mary hungered for the fruit of the Spirit (Galatians 5:22–23). Her creative mind focused on the only person who could fill her craving. She served by humbling herself before Jesus, her Redeemer. Sitting at the feet of Jesus and listening to His words brought:

- Love
- Joy
- Peace
- Patience
- Kindness
- Goodness
- Faithfulness
- Self-control

Although Scripture does not elaborate on Martha's reaction to what Jesus said, it must have been a moment of truth for her. Becoming real with a situation is never easy, but it allows self-examination and acceptance. Then healing may begin.

Reflections

What do you need to do now to become real?

*Lord, help us to communicate
our true feelings to others.*

CHAPTER 8

Breaking the Cycle

*In this you greatly rejoice, though now for a little while
you may have had to suffer grief in all kinds of trials.
These have come so that your faith—of greater worth than
gold, which perishes even though refined by fire— may be
proved genuine and may result in praise, glory and honor
when Jesus Christ is revealed.*
—1 Peter 1:6–7

A story is told about an African boy who takes a gourd,
dries it, hollows it out, and then puts a little hole in the
gourd just large enough for a monkey to reach through with
his hand. Then the boy ties a rope to the gourd and to the
base of a tree. Inside the gourd, the boy puts something the
curious monkey wants, like a chicken bone. Then he walks
off a distance to wait.

Soon a monkey explores the gourd, shakes it, and spies the
bone inside. He reaches his hand into the gourd and grabs the
bone. However, when he tries to remove the bone, he discovers
he can't get it out because the bone has become wedged in the
narrow opening. He pulls and pulls, but it will not come out.

Then, because the monkey's sole concentration is on the
bone, the little African boy walks up and catches him. The
monkey screams and screams, yanking on the chicken bone,
but he won't let go of his prize. The monkey is caught.

If we have been the victims of verbal and emotional abuse
for years, it has probably affected our lives in many ways. In
our relationships with others, we may suffer silently with the

pent-up anger building inside of us. We hold onto our anger, and we refuse to let go of our "chicken bone." Or we may tend to overreact, lose our cool, and act out the role of the abuser. If this is the case, we need to pinpoint the triggers that set off our actions and see them for what they are. In order to break this vicious cycle, we need to become aware of exactly what is happening.

We aren't capable of changing on our own. First and foremost we need to ask for God's help in order to break the vicious cycle of verbal abuse. He may direct us to seek the counsel of friends, family members, and/or professional therapists—whatever it takes to make us let go of our "chicken bones" and be set free.

MOST OF HER LIFE, Susan waited in hope that her mother's verbal abuse would end, but that moment never arrived. With God's help, she was able to break that cycle, forgive her mother, and never abuse her two sons.

La Jolla Memories
Susan Titus Osborn

Every August while my sons were growing up, my mother rented a hotel room at the beautiful La Valencia Hotel in La Jolla, California. The hotel was located on the beach, and we could walk out the back gate right onto the sand.

My sons, Richard and Mike, looked forward to a week at the beach with their grandmother and me. I prayed that my boys would never see the tarnished side of her drinking problem. Usually she behaved around her grandsons.

During one such vacation when the boys were 12 and 14, we'd had a wonderful time until the last night. Mother started drinking at lunch, continued during dinner, until she couldn't walk on her own. Richard put his arms around her and guided her back to the hotel.

Tears filled my eyes, and I told myself, *Stay calm. Mother just lost her husband. Maybe she's afraid to return home to an empty house. Perhaps that's what triggered her drinking tonight.* Nevertheless, that was no excuse for her behavior.

"I don't know why you married that man. He's a loser," Mom slurred.

I was seething inside by this point, but I didn't want her badmouthing the boys' father in front of them. We had developed a few problems in our marriage, but I didn't think it was something Mother should be discussing with the boys. I regretted that I had previously confided in her.

I tried to change the subject. "Mother, we have really enjoyed our week with you."

"Yes, we have," chimed in Richard. "Thanks for inviting us."

"Susan never listens to me," Mother obnoxiously complained to her grandsons. "Why is she always trying to change the subject, and your father never comes with you. Does he think he's too good to spend a vacation with me?"

"He's in Washington on business," I replied, defending him, although it seemed like he was always in Washington on business. "He can't get away easily from his work, and he thought we'd like some special time with you."

"You call this week special time? The three of you spent most of your time at the beach on the boogie boards I bought you. You didn't spend any time with me."

Mike just stood there wide-eyed. He didn't say a word, but Richard came to our defense. "Grandma, we played games with you, went shopping with you, and took walks with you. We only spent a little time at the beach. And besides, you know we love the beach."

I chimed in, "Mother, you told the boys you invited us so we could spend time at the beach. None of us feel like we neglected you and—"

"Oh, what do you know?" Mother interrupted. "What do you care about my feelings? You just spend my money and take off and leave me."

I tried to sound stern. "That's not true. We love you, and we enjoyed this vacation with you. Don't ruin it for us."

At that point, Mother opened her hotel room door and walked in. We went down the hall to ours, and I breathed a sigh of relief.

The next day, Mother didn't say a word about our conversation the previous evening. I doubt that she remembered any of it. We dropped her at the airport and drove home.

All of us were quiet for the first few miles, and then Richard said, "You told us that Grandma had a drinking problem. And you told us she said hurtful things to you over the years, but you never explained how bad these situations were. I guess you didn't want to worry us."

"We didn't understand why you walked on eggshells around her and tried to keep her happy all the time," said Mike, "but now we know why."

Richard reached over and touched my shoulder. "It must be hard having a mom like Grandma. I'm sure glad we have a mom like you."

Tears filled my eyes, and I blinked them back. "Thanks, boys. I try to be the best mom I can. I love you both, and I promise I'll never treat you like I've been treated by Grandma."

Mike smiled. "Don't worry, Mom. You're the best mom in the world."

"Mike was able to call what he saw with Susan 'walking on eggshells,'" states Jeenie. "Actually, it consisted of Susan covering up her mother's drinking and verbal abuse, as well as her husband's verbal abuse.

"In these instances, it worked. She was honoring her mother and husband while shielding her sons from the reality of the ugliness. It's called 'being godly.'

"Susan could have bad-mouthed her husband and

Wounded by Words

mother and probably felt justified in being honest. However, because Susan did what was right, her sons were able to open their eyes and see truth. The boys were able 'to call a spade a spade,' yet love their grandmother in spite of her inadequacies. God always rewards the one who honors."

DEANNA DEALT WITH AN abusive parent most of her life until she, too, discovered how to break the cycle of verbal abuse before it affected the lives of her husband and children.

Walls of Protection
Deanna Barnes

My father raised his voice. "This is a rotten place. What is that slop you feed us, anyway?" The gentle woman who owned his board-and-care home said nothing as his verbal abuse continued.

Then my father turned to me. After several snide comments about how good my life was compared to his, he said, "You think my mother went to hell, don't you?"

The stabbing words startled me. I recognized his comments as another technique to attack the deepest core of my heart—my faith. As a mature 45-year-old woman, I faced the truth. He had insulted me in similar ways over the years.

For months before this incident, I had been trying to help my elderly father recover from physical, mental, and financial breakdown. When he spoke those words, pictures from childhood flashed into my mind. I remembered being seven years old, huddled in a back room with my younger sisters, listening to this man scream abusive words at our mother—just because she wanted to go to church.

Back in the present, I found myself the target of his abuse. Would I allow his negativity to continue to transfer to me and affect my family? I had to make a choice to build walls of protection—one of the most difficult tasks of my life.

A mixture of good memories with my dad added to my anguish. He spent time with me as a child on fishing trips at dawn and camping under the stars. Also he taught me to draw, showed me how to garden, and cared for me when I was sick.

In contrast, his angry outbursts frightened me. Cruel words and abusive actions kept my family in turmoil. When I was 14, my parents divorced, and after that I had limited communication with my father.

During those lonely years, friends at church helped me find comfort and love from my heavenly Father. I often hid in my room, listened to Christian music, and poured out my sorrow in prayer. In my journal I wrote Scripture verses of promise such as *"Wait on the Lord: be of good courage, and he shall strengthen thine heart: wait, I say, on the Lord"* (Psalm 27:14 KJV). God protected me and made it possible for me to begin to heal.

As time went on, however, I realized that I still had unresolved issues. Then one New Year's Eve, I heard a minister speak of the destructive consequences of an unforgiving attitude. "If you won't forgive," he said, "you will only harm yourself." At the close of the message, I fell to my knees to ask God to help me forgive my father. The acid of bitterness vanished from my heart.

Years passed. Circumstances brought my father back into my life. His second wife—weary of his verbal and emotional abuse—divorced him. He lost his home due to his financial decisions. He wrecked his car. Physical and mental illness further complicated his situation. As his life unraveled, my sister and I tried to help. We took time from our families and our jobs, spending hours on the phone with doctors and social workers. We traveled to the hospital to meet with caregivers. We invested our own money to provide necessities for our father. Despite our efforts, he continued his downward spiral.

When I became the object of his verbal abuse, his words left me shaken and confused. Irrational thoughts pounded my mind. *Maybe I am selfish because I do not want to care for this man anymore. I should be willing to do anything to help him. Maybe if I do enough he will change into the person I have always hoped he would be.*

Finally, with God's help, I realized that this situation demanded that I break the cycle. My pastor and my friends helped me accept the fact that my father's words and actions were destroying my life and my relationship with my own family. I learned that I could not expect a normal father/daughter relationship with this man. I had the right to say no and to set limits without feeling guilty.

Other resources were available for his care. The time had arrived to build a wall of protection to stop the cycle of abuse. For weeks, I struggled with my decision. Then the incident at the board-and-care home brought everything into focus. I knew I had to draw the line immediately.

My hands trembled as I confronted him. "I warned you that if you didn't change your behavior, I would withdraw from your life." I turned from his taunting, ridiculing eyes. "I'm leaving now."

Seeing my resolve, he switched to a pitiful whine. "How can I ask you to forgive me again?"

"I do forgive you now, as I have in the past, but I am not going to let you speak abusively to me any longer." I kissed him good-bye, tears pouring down my cheeks. My heart wrenched with sorrow as I drove away.

After my decision, my father did quite well under the supervision of others. I maintained some degree of contact with him on special occasions. However, the guard around my inner self and my family stayed in place.

Two years later, he suffered congestive heart failure. I rushed to his bedside in the intensive care unit. There he asked me to forgive him for everything he had put me through over the years. It was a precious gift. He died the next day.

Grief enveloped me, but the sweet presence of God never left. His gracious mercy and tender love provided every need.

Looking back on the complex journey with my father, I realize that building walls of protection kept my life and my marriage intact. The walls had enabled me to break the cycle of verbal abuse. Today our sons are raising their children in Christian homes, filled with peace and joy.

The cycle of abuse broke under boundaries of love and forgiveness. Deanna learned she no longer needed to put up with abuse.

● ● ●

"Deanna's story resonated big time with me," Jeenie remembers. "Vividly I recall my father screaming at my mom, 'I'm not going to eat this slop.' With one full swoop, he threw his plate across the room. As a small child, I watched in horror as the meat, mashed potatoes, and gravy slowly slid down the yellow kitchen wall.

"Years later, while visiting me, he again yelled, 'I'm not going to eat this slop.'

"I responded, 'Dad, I broiled the pork chops the way you like and fixed a lovely dinner for you. However, if you don't like it, you need not eat it.' Then I left the room."

We must realize that some people are toxic to us. When they behave obnoxiously, then strong boundaries must be established in order for us to function in an emotionally healthy manner.

ABUSIVE SITUATIONS ARE ALSO found in the workplace. These can be difficult to handle, especially if the abuser is your superior and your job and paycheck depend on him.

Deer in the Headlights
Neelie Williams

I had the deer-in-the-headlights look as my principal leaned across his desk and continued his harangue. He'd called me into his office on the pretext of discussing a student, but his purpose was twofold.

There had been gossip rampant on campus about his flirtatious behavior with another teacher. I'd not been privy to the gossip at first, but late one afternoon, I overheard a conversation and asked questions. The answers appalled me. It seemed our married principal and a married teacher were having a fling.

I left the gossip session and walked to my in box near the teacher's lounge. I passed the principal on the way and barely acknowledged his presence. Within the span of an hour, our paths crossed three times. My embarrassment at knowing his professed wrongdoings kept me from eye contact. He noticed the change in my usual outgoing behavior. I wasn't rude, just quiet.

Therefore, when he could drum up an excuse, he called me into the inner sanctum along with his secretary as a witness to our meeting. He folded his hands, fingers steeple-like. "I want to know what's bothering you. You're usually more upbeat. I detect a note of unfriendliness here."

"I apologize, sir. It's been a long day." I shifted in my chair.

"It has been that." He leaned forward. "I want to know what's bothering you." A scowl crossed his face. "Tell me now."

My eyes met his glare. "I'm fine, sir."

"No, you aren't fine." He spit out the last word. "Something is wrong."

"I really don't wish to discuss anything with you right now, sir. It's late. We're both tired." I slid forward in my chair as if to leave and smiled over my shoulder at his secretary, who stood as a sentry.

"Look, if there's something going on at my campus, I want to know." His voice rose. "I don't care if it's late, and you're tired." His hand slapped the desktop. "If you know something I need to know, then spit it out."

Heat flamed my cheeks. "Sir, I have never had to discuss anything like this with an adult male. I choose not to." I stood.

"Sit down." He rose from his chair and stepped around the desk, towering over me. "I think we need to hash this out."

"No, sir. That's not a good idea." I regained my composure. I'd had enough of this man's attitude. "There's gossip rampant, but I'm not part of it."

He looked stunned. "Gossip?" He thundered, "What story are you spreading?"

"Sir, I am not part of the gossip," my voice quivered. "I have no story to spread."

"Then get your stuff and get off my campus now." His angry glare bore into me. The veins in his forehead bulged. "And keep your mouth shut from now on."

I drew myself up to my five-foot-two stature and quietly left his office, my insides quivering like jelly. Without shedding a nervous tear, I made it to the confines of my car and drove out of the parking lot. I had to pull into a gas station to calm myself down. His verbal abuse had resurfaced many arguments I'd had during my marriage to an alcoholic. Feelings I thought I'd long ago dealt with crept into my brain. I shivered and shook for quite some time, then surrendered to prayer. With God's guidance, I made it home.

It took me days to regain my composure on campus when the principal was in the vicinity. He'd targeted me because I was usually frank with him on school issues. His obvious disdain permeated the air when we passed. Other teachers noticed. Soon scuttlebutt had it I'd been rude to him. Those rumors were laughed at by my friends who knew me. Still, it stung.

Wounded by Words

I learned he'd been verbally abusive to some young, new teachers, so I made up my mind his behavior needed to stop. I knew, given the chance, he would grind up those under his command. I met with the assistant superintendent and gave her the complete details of our conversation. To my surprise, she already knew about the relationship.

"I will remove him as your evaluator." She scribbled notes on a pad. "I will also see that you have no more one-on-one sessions with him."

"Thank you." Relief flooded through me. "This is an answer to prayer. I didn't come here lightly. In my 30-year career, I've never had to file a grievance or make a complaint against a fellow employee."

"I understand. We appreciate your candor." She faced me. "And this behavior needs to stop. It's not healthy for the school."

A message was sent to the principal, and we no longer had any reason for contact. I continued my school year, avoiding him as much as possible. At the end of the year, a small party was given for those of us retiring. He refused to attend, an unheard-of precedent. His childish behavior was noted by the faculty, and their respect dropped another notch.

In my opinion, verbal abuse takes a physical and emotional toll as violent and severe as physical abuse. Learning to stand up and not be a victim is a hard lesson. But it can be learned. Evaluate the situation for what it is: a selfish boor making himself more important than what he is. Decide if what is being said is necessary for you to hear. If it is, explain you'll listen when the conversation can be held in a more pleasant manner. Walk out. Don't subject yourself to needless derogatory remarks. The accuser might even be right in some instances, but his manner of speaking, tone, and body language need not frighten or intimidate you. If you are uncomfortable, leave. Explain your actions later.

Do not allow another person to take control of your emotional well-being. God is our Protector. Call upon Him in times of trouble. Pray for guidance. Deal with the accuser when you can handle the situation, in God's timing, not the accuser's. Take a trusted witness. The presence of a person on your side can put a damper on the ire of the accuser.

Be smart. Be wary. Don't be blindsided. Don't deal with the situation when you are not at your best. Be armed. Pray. Then step in and be in control. You can. After all, God is on your side!

"Neelie was one brave woman," Jeenie concurs. It is vital in our confrontation that we are gentle and firm. Being only gentle will accomplish nothing—it's a cop-out. Conversely, firmness alone usually comes off as an overly aggressive stance. Neither is emotionally healthy or godly when used alone. However, when we combine the two, firmness and gentleness, it often accomplishes a great deal.

Even though Neelie did not change the principal's behavior, with God's help she could be in control of her own reaction.

Dialogue in the Dark
Charles R. Brown

It's so dark here.
I'm afraid.
The Lord is your light.
Light?
And your salvation.
From what?
The darkness; the fear.
But, I am so feeble,

weak-kneed,
wobbly-headed.
The Lord is your stronghold.
Why fear?
The enemy wants to attack me.
My heart trembles.
Wait.
You are not listening.
The Lord is your light.
The Lord is your salvation.
The Lord is your stronghold.
If you will believe that;
if you will claim that;
confidence will invade
your fearful heart.
Who are you, anyway?
I AM.
Yes, Lord!

The Samaritan woman is an example of someone who lived in the dark until Jesus shed light on her darkness. Her story can be found in John 4:4–42.

Weary from His long journey, Jesus rested by a well. The noon sun beat down, while off in the distance the lone figure of a woman approached. Even though a water supply existed in Sychar, she traveled a half-mile to the well of Jacob. William Barclay's *Daily Study Bible* states, "May it be that she was so much of a moral outcast that the women even drove her away from the village well, and she had to come here to draw water?"

Scripture doesn't give us her name, but rather describes her as "the Samaritan woman at the well," a woman ostracized and expecting no opportunity for change in her lifetime. As an adulteress, her dishonorable reputation built walls of isolation.

It took the *sound* of Jesus's voice to shatter that wall—a kind, gentle voice; the voice of a Jewish rabbi.

Jesus asked her, *"Will you give me a drink?"* (John 4:7). Startled, she struggled over the issue. Jews did not speak with Samaritans for they considered them impure because of intermarriages outside of the Jewish race. When she looked into His noncritical eyes, she felt drawn to Him.

"You are a Jew and I am a Samaritan woman. How can you ask me for a drink?" (John 4:9).

Jesus explained that He offers living water. She wrestled with the concept. For her mind only knew of earthly water that quenched physical thirst. But Jesus spoke of a spiritual thirst.

> He told her, *"Go, call your husband and come back."*
> *"I have no husband,"* she replied.
> Jesus said to her, *"You are right when you say you have no husband. The fact is, you have had five husbands, and the man you now have is not your husband. What you have just said is quite true."*
> —John 4:16–18

Amazed at His knowledge, she asked Him if He were a prophet. Then even more amazingly, He spoke to her of a time when both Jews and Samaritans would worship in spirit and truth.

> The woman said, *"I know that Messiah"* (called Christ) *"is coming. When he comes, he will explain everything to us."*
> Then Jesus declared, *"I who speak to you am he."*
> —John 4:25–26

As a result, she returned to her town and testified, *"Come see a man who told me everything I ever did. Could this be the Christ?"* (John 4:29).

Jesus stayed with the Samaritans for two days. Because of His words to the woman, many became believers.

The compassion of Christ is certainly demonstrated in this story. The cycle of mistrust and hate had gone on between the Samaritans and Jews for many years. Yet, here is Christ revealing the truth to an ostracized woman among her own people. She could have taken her water jar and gone back into town without speaking a word about the Jewish rabbi who spoke to her. Yet, she chose to take a chance and spoke of a stranger whose actions demonstrated love for all people. She declared the truth—the Messiah had come.

What was evident in the Samaritan woman's actions when she saw the light of Christ?

- Her willingness to change.
- Her truthfulness.
- Her ability to recognize that God loved her regardless of her past.
- Her courage to face those who rejected her.

We can take courage from her example as we deal with abusive people and situations today.

Reflections

Describe what you might do to break the cycle of abuse in your life.

*Lord, I know that alone I cannot break
the cycle of abuse. I need Your help.*

CHAPTER 9

Believing in Myself

For I know the plans I have for you,"
declares the LORD, "plans to prosper you and not
not to harm you, plans to give you hope and a future.
—Jeremiah 29:11

Before you build a house, the first thing you need to do is develop a plan. You may use an architect and a builder, or you may come up with ideas yourself, but you definitely need a plan. Likewise, God has developed a plan for your life, and it's your responsibility to accept that plan and determine ways to follow it.

A builder checks the land before he begins construction. You don't want your house built on the shifting sand that Jesus describes:

> *"Therefore everyone who hears these words of mine and puts them into practice is like a wise man who built his house on the rock. The rain came down, the streams rose, and the winds blew and beat against that house; yet it did not fall, because it had its foundation on the rock. But everyone who hears these words of mine and does not put them into practice is like a foolish man who built his house on sand. The rain came down, the streams rose, and the winds blew and beat against that house, and it fell with a great crash."*
> *—Matthew 7:24–27*

When the actual building begins, the first thing put in place is the foundation. But before the concrete slab is poured, the builder needs to develop a floor plan, measure the rooms, and lay wooden forms. Much planning and work goes into the project before the actual construction begins.

Likewise we need to let God lay down a solid foundation for our lives. Our previous foundation, our self-confidence and self-esteem, may have been eroded by constant exposure to verbal abuse. When we come to the realization that we do not deserve to be put down with demeaning, caustic words, we can begin to rebuild our lives, using God's plan. Our foundation will be built on Jesus Christ. Through study of His Word, prayer, and counseling, our distorted image of ourselves begins to change. Gradually our hope and faith are renewed.

"Starting a quarrel is like breaching a dam; so drop the matter before a dispute breaks out" (Proverbs 17:14).

WORDS THAT HURT followed Kay into adulthood, and she questioned, "Why does one harsh criticism from my mother reduce me to a frightened little girl, desperate for love and approval?"

Words That Hurt
Kay L. Lee

I hung up the phone and felt my stomach churn as my mother's words rang in my ears. "How could you forget to call me? You'll be sorry someday when your son is grown."

Why—after all these years—does Mom still have the power to demolish me? It doesn't matter that I'm a 35-year-old woman with a loving husband, a woman who had a successful career before trading it in to manage three small children. How silly of me! I actually hoped she'd encourage me as I battle exhaustion, caring for my children, I thought. Instead, I'm the one in "trouble" for not calling according to her timetable.

In the past, the anger I felt after an upsetting conversation with Mom would engulf me to the point where I would become out of control. But now, as I felt rage welling up in me, I knew what I had to do: Drop to my knees and beg the Lord for self-control. Instantly, I pulled from memory the verse I'd learned to get myself back on track when dealing with Mom's critical tongue: *"Then you will know the truth, and the truth will set you free"* (John 8:32). God comforted me by reminding me of the "truth" of the situation. I hadn't done anything that would make a normal mother angry.

I'm a people pleaser by nature. As a child, Mom encouraged this characteristic by rewarding behavior that catered to her needs. If I cleaned the house, fixed dinner, rubbed her back, or answered her beck and call, I got "strokes" from her—something I desperately craved. I learned her rules and set out to do whatever it took to "keep Mom loving me." But unfortunately, her rules changed daily. I quickly learned I could do all the work she wanted, but she could still withdraw her love for no apparent reason. I was only as good as the last thing I did for her, and even that depended on her mood.

Once in the sixth grade, after I had won 12 awards for various field day and academic contests, my mother and a friend picked me up after school. I ran to Mom, bursting with my achievements, only to hear her say, "Don't be so pleased with yourself. No one cares about your stupid awards." Minutes later, Mom bragged to her friend about her talented daughter.

If I called my mother on her inconsistent behavior, she'd scream hysterically, "After all I've done for you, how can you treat me like this? I hate you!"

Through all the verbal abuse, I never gave up trying to win my mother's love. I merely tried harder. *If I just do more for her, she'll finally love me,* I thought.

By the time I left for college, I felt intensely insecure and constantly searched for ways to fill my insatiable need for achievement. I felt as though I had to earn my friends daily. But the worst abuse was that which I heaped on myself when I made an honest mistake. It would take me months to get over feeling like I'd failed.

I dreaded Christmas break because I'd have to go home. My fourth stepfather was an abusive alcoholic, and he and Mom had intense fights that resulted in him leaving for weeks at a time. During those periods, my mother would be extremely nice and look to me as her counselor. Then, without comment, she and my stepfather would patch up their differences, and we would be back together as a family. If I didn't welcome him back with open arms, I would be labeled a troublemaker. The mixed messages were confusing and devastating.

To my surprise, when I went home for Christmas, my stepfather was gone—for good. Mom explained that a friend had invited her to church, and she had accepted Jesus. A Bible now sat on a table in our home, and Mom promised to clean up her life.

I had grown up going to Sunday School, but I never knew much about God. I decided that if He could change Mom, even temporarily, then I'd better dig into religion. I joined a college Bible study, prayed, and learned that "religion" wasn't the issue. Jesus wanted to have a personal relationship with me. He cared for me unconditionally. That was a new concept for me, so when I discovered I didn't have to earn His love, I thought, *Where do I sign up?*

I wish I could say Mom's life truly changed after her encounter with the Lord, but she hasn't let God transform her life. I quickly learned I had to look at the Source of my faith—Jesus, the Sinless One—rather than at my mother's example. Mom did lead me to Him, however, and for that I'm forever grateful.

Through Christian therapy, prayer, and Bible study, I found that the key to breaking Mom's grip on my life was forgiveness. But how could I forgive her for years of abuse? How could I let go of my anger? It was only through the power of God that I finally decided to forgive Mom. And once I made that decision, I felt my rage start to melt away.

After 17 years, there are still moments when I fall into the "victim mentality." But a supportive husband, close personal friends, and a journal help me defend myself against the void Mom leaves in my life.

I'll always feel disappointment at the lack of relationship with her. But as my healing has progressed, I've started to like myself more. I keep time spent around Mom to a minimum, and my day doesn't start until I've spent time with God. I know daily prayer and Scripture reading are the only ways to keep my self-esteem. As I've grown as a Christian, my need to please everyone has diminished. I've learned not to feel guilty for not measuring up to an unrealistic, self-imposed standard.

Because of the Lord's help, I can honestly say I love Mom and want the best for her. By keeping God paramount in my life I know I won't repeat the cycle of my upbringing with my children. Healing from a hurtful past is a lifelong project. But God promises that with His help, I have the power to stay on track, and I believe Him.

● ● ●

The antics of Kay's mother remind Jeenie of a borderline personality disorder (BPD). Borderlines can be sweet and horrid. People never know where they stand with them. And, as Kay suggested, it's very confusing.

One incident comes to Jeenie's mind of a borderline client to whom, while in therapy, Jeenie delicately suggested that change may be needed. The client screamed obscenities, raged, called Jeenie names, and blamed others. Leaving the office, she slammed the door so hard the windows shook.

When she walked out, her husband asked, "See what I have to live with?"

After a week, Jeenie telephoned and she refused to talk to her. After a few days she called, apologizing profusely, and told Jeenie that she was the best thing since sliced bread. "I want to send you flowers," she gushed.

Jeenie explained, "You are welcome back. However, I will be honest as well as supportive."

The childhood background of a borderline is usually one of abuse. And, somewhere in their childlike thoughts, they decided they would never be abused again. So, in turn, they became the abuser. The borderline personality is a defense against pain. Seldom can a person with BPD be reasoned with, and rarely will he or she take medication to remedy the disorder.

Diagnostic criteria from American Psychiatric Association (DSM IV-TR®) gives a few of the characteristics of borderlines: Avoid real or imagined abandonment; unstable and intense interpersonal relationships with extreme impulsivity; unstable moods; chronic feelings of emptiness; inappropriate, intense anger, and so on.

Kay mentioned that her mom accepted Christ. However, there wasn't long-lasting change. "God changes our hearts, not our personalities. That's our job," states Jeenie.

LOOKING BACK AT the most difficult time of her life, Karri realized that she had a choice. She could remain bitter and depressed or she could allow God to heal her. She chose to become a daughter of the King.

Daughters of the King
Karri Ashley

At the close of a morning session at a Christian women's retreat the director said, "Take your notebooks and Bibles and go outside to spend time meditating on God's love and mercy."

We all went in different directions to locate secluded places to be alone with God in this beautiful mountain setting. Leaning over a fence, I looked down at the dried-up creek bed where pure white boulders caught my eye. I silently prayed. *Lord, I'm so thankful that my daughter and I are together here. Sue has become a wonderful daughter, friend, and wife. I know it is because of Your grace and mercy.*

Out of the corner of my eye I saw movement. I smiled as I watched my 36-year-old daughter walking along the path toward me. I closed my eyes and remembered the past—

After the SIDS death of Sue's baby sister, Kim, I'd returned to college and taken a course in key punching. Six weeks later I'd received a certificate of completion. At home I threw my certificate in a kitchen drawer and forgot about it.

Then a few weeks later, my husband, Hank, confessed, "I lied to you, Karri, when you asked if I was seeing another woman. I didn't tell you sooner about Elaine, because if it didn't work out, I wouldn't have anyone."

The foundation of my "solid" marriage had turned to quicksand. I sank into hopelessness. Soon after this, my sister called and said, "Karri, a position in the key-punch department where I work has opened up."

I applied and was hired. God placed me in a Christian company surrounded by strong, supportive people when I most needed it. I worked there for a year. Surprisingly, Hank entered counseling with me. My marriage improved. I thought we had a chance, so I left my job and continued taking medical assisting college courses.

Words of betrayal from my husband had become common. Yet, I believed our marriage would survive. Then Hank's work placed him on a special assignment in Palm Springs. Several weeks later he called to say, "Karri, I'd like you and the kids to come join me for the Fourth of July weekend."

During that time he lavished us with attention. On our trip back home, I felt like I'd experienced a weekend in paradise. His words, *I love you,* echoed in my mind.

I was shocked when a week later Hank came home and announced, "I am leaving. I want a divorce."

Tears streamed down my cheeks as I looked into my husband's eyes and wondered where the man I loved had gone.

I listened to his words and prayed that I'd wake up from this nightmare. Silently, I thanked God that my children were not home. Sue was at church summer camp, and Lee was on a Boy Scout outing.

Hank continued, "I've seen an attorney, and if you fight me, you'll lose everything. You can file for divorce since you are the woman."

No way, I thought, *I didn't betray our vows*. Shaking off fear I stated, "You're the one who wants a divorce, so you'll have to file. I have one question, though. Why did you tell me last week that you loved me?"

"I thought maybe I could try again, but on the way home tonight, I stopped to call Elaine. She needs me."

"Are you saying the kids and I don't need you?"

"If you want to keep the kids, Karri, don't fight me."

"If that's the way you feel, then good-bye, Hank."

In that brief but awful moment I understood I must let go. For a year and a half I'd stayed in my marriage, hoping that Hank's affair would end. As I watched him walk to his car and drive off, I knew our 17-year marriage was over.

A few days later a Christian friend called and gave me the name of an attorney. Even though Hank filed, I needed to protect myself and my children.

My tears flowed. "Lord, I don't know how I'll survive. Help me to accept that my marriage is over. Where do I go from here?" Yet, as I thought about it, I realized that over the last year and a half before Hank left that God had prepared me for that time.

The 7 years I spent as a single mom were not easy. I had to work long, hard hours and often my adolescent son and daughter felt alone. We struggled physically, emotionally, and spiritually—

"Mom, Mom." My daughter's voice brought me back to the present. I looked up into her smiling face.

"Hi, Sue. Come join me." We sat down together on a bench, and I gave her a hug. The fresh smell of pine trees permeated the air, filling me with joy. I looked at Sue and said, "God has given us so many blessings."

"Yes," she replied, "but Mom, there were times I didn't think I'd make it after Dad left."

"I know, but through all the adversity, God taught us to trust Him and to forgive."

"I have, Mom. And today I'm so grateful for my wonderful husband and daughters."

"I, too, am blessed with a Christian husband, one who often tells me, "I love you more today than yesterday.""

Sue and I bowed our heads in prayer, "Lord, You delivered us from emotional abuse and abandonment. Thank You for teaching us to believe in ourselves as daughters of the King."

● ● ●

An old song from her childhood, "Beauty for Ashes," echoes in Jeenie's mind. It talks about how the Lord gives joy for sorrow. Sadness and oppression are exchanged for rest. God does not promise us a second marriage, a good income, or excellent health, but He does promise us His peace. And what can be greater?

What a great comfort is this promise: *"Peace I leave with you; my peace I give you. I do not give to you as the world gives. Do not let your hearts be troubled and do not be afraid"* (John 14:27).

Ice Skater
Connie L. Peters

There seems to be a part of me
Afraid to relax and smile,
Afraid to say that I'm OK
I'm God's beloved child.
Like a poor ice skater
Shuffling on the rink,

Cautious with each step
Caring what others think.

It seems I'm always wary
That I'll stumble and fall flat
That others will trip over me,
Landing with a splat.

You want me to skate strong, Lord,
Throw my head back in the wind,
Smile and enjoy myself
As I glide along with friends.

Help me to skate boldly
With a confident stride,
Knowing you are with me
Skating by my side.

Embracing Grace
Candy Abbott

Babysitting at my daughter's one Thursday night, I sat snuggled in a blanket, enjoying a movie in the living room while my grandchildren lay upstairs sound asleep. I looked up when the front door opened and Kim and her husband entered.

"How was Bible study?" I asked Wyatt, who came through the door first.

"Ha!" He gave a bitter snort. "Better ask Kim."

What in the world? I threw off the blanket and bolted upright. One look at my daughter's face, and I knew she was terribly upset. "What happened?"

The events of the evening gushed out of her like water from a fire hydrant. Apparently their small-group discussion on forgiveness and grace had deteriorated when Kim quoted portions of the lesson instead of being sympathetic to one woman's problems.

"See?" the woman shouted and pointed her finger at Kim. "That's just what I mean. Its preachy people like you who drive people like *me* out of the church!"

While Wyatt attempted to regain a sense of proper perspective, Kim became all the more agitated. "She pounced on me, Mom, when all I did was try to help." Kim crossed her arms. "Now, I'm not proud of this, but you know what I did? I turned my back to her and never said another word the rest of the evening."

I didn't comment at the time, but I came home troubled, not only about the incident, but because I was aware, for the first time, of how little grace I could see in my beautiful daughter's adult life. A perfectionist by nature, she always seemed to be striving, pressing, trying to prove something illusive to herself, with only fleeting moments of happiness, never truly content. More often than she cared to admit, Kim lived in a state of controlled rage, like a pot of boiling water with the lid clamped on tightly.

The next day, as I prayed for Kim, the Lord gave me a flashback of her teenage years. Often as I had tried to offer grace and optimism, she had spewed out, "I'm not *like* you, Mom, sweet and nice. I'll never be like you. I don't *want* to be like you." In essence, she was not rejecting me so much as God's loving-kindness and grace, preferring to work things out on her own, usually with "justice" in mind. Why hadn't I seen it before?

I dashed off an email to her at work with my revelation. *Maybe I should have waited,* I thought as soon as I hit Send. After all, as a fifth-grade teacher, she could be having a difficult day with her students, and I didn't want to add more stress. But it was too late. The message was on its way:

Hon, I believe I may know why it is so difficult for you to comprehend and embrace grace. It isn't up to you to obtain justice—that's God's job. Your job is to love. The Lord reminded me of the many negative things you said about yourself as a teenager. It is possible that those words constituted a verbal curse, something no one would do intentionally but that the devil can use as "permission" to block you from God's grace and ability to sense His love. If you agree, you will need to repent of your words aloud (because they were spoken aloud); then ask the Lord to replace your negativity with His grace. The timing is crucial as these are impressionable years for your kids, and it is your responsibility as a wife and mother to set the emotional tone of your household. When you begin practicing grace toward yourself and others, you'll be surprised at how life's pressures (from rebellious students to family squabbles) will seem less stressful, and you'll be able to enjoy the rest of your life.

Kim called Sunday afternoon. "Oh, Mom, you won't believe the chain of events that happened this weekend—and it all had to do with what you told me Friday."

Surely, she couldn't mean my email. "You mean Thursday night?"

"No, Mom, what you said in your email. I knew you were right but, to be honest, I was nowhere ready to repent on Friday night. Then on Saturday, Bonnie came and picked up the kids, Wyatt was hunting, and I had some unexpected quiet time. I put in a preacher's CD, and—Mom, you won't believe it! I can't remember the exact words, but he asked something like, 'Did you know that things you say in your youth can have a negative impact on your whole adult life?' Talk about getting my attention! And then he went on to cover everything you said in your email, almost word for word—from the need to repent *aloud*, to my responsibility to speak to my children in love, right down to justice being the Lord's responsibility."

By the time the CD ended, Kim knew she had encountered the living God in her living room. Repenting aloud, she asked

Christ to fill her to overflowing with grace and loving-kindness.

Kim had never sounded more relaxed. She said, "Mom, I feel like a new person, and I slept the whole night through. I hadn't done that since my first pregnancy!"

The preacher was right. If we allow our thoughts to defeat us and then give birth to negative ideas through our words, our actions will follow suit. Our words have tremendous power. And whether we want to or not, we give life to what we're saying, either good or bad.

Kim forgave all who had offended her over the years—including the woman at Bible study. With her new attitude of living a life of forgiveness, I can only imagine what grace she will bring to her household—and to next week's Bible study meeting.

How deadly is perfectionism—not only for the person, but for those around her because the perfectionist has impossible standards for everyone. With Kim, the fury raged inside her because she was unable to live up to her own strict principles. She could not show mercy to herself or others.

Perfectionism stops us often from trying because we know there will not be a perfect outcome. So, we give up entirely.

God is a God of mercy. He does not demand perfection—only faithfulness. When Kim was able to look at the root issue of her youthful rage, she could repent and break free.

The Old Testament story of Esther, in which a poor orphan girl became queen of Persia, contains drama, intrigue, and romance. It reads like a good suspense novel. It shows one man's hatred toward another, but it also involves courage in the face of circumstances beyond human control. Esther willingly risked her life to save her Jewish people.

Then Haman said to King Xerxes [Zersees], "There is a certain people dispersed and scattered among the peoples

in all the provinces of your kingdom whose customs are
different from those of all other people and who do not
obey the king's laws; it is not in the king's best interest to
tolerate them."

—Esther 3:8

Haman, a man promoted by the king above all the royal officials, smiled as he left the king. The king's words echoed in his mind. *Do with the people as you please* (v. 11).

Haman thought his evil scheme would soon bring the revenge he sought. *That fool! Didn't he know that I have found favor with the king? I will destroy Mordecai—the Jew who refused to bow before me at the king's gate. His stupidity will destroy all the Jewish people.*

Dispatchers delivered the order that all Jews—young and old, women and children—would be annihilated on the 13th day of the 12th month. Esther did not yet know of the edict, but news reached her that her cousin Mordecai sat at the king's gate in sackcloth and ashes—a sign of mourning. When her own parents had died, Mordecai had adopted Esther and raised her like a daughter. She'd come to know him as a man of compassion, a man of action, and one who walked with the Lord. Distressed, Esther wondered what could be troubling Mordecai.

Esther sent Hathach, one of the king's eunuchs, to Mordecai. Soon Hathach returned with a copy of the king's edict regarding the annihilation of the Jews. He also brought a plea from Mordecai for Esther to petition the king for mercy.

Esther's anxiety grew by the minute. *What should I do? Going before the king without being summoned could mean death.* After much deliberation Esther sent a reply to Mordecai:

"Go, gather together all the Jews who are in Susa, and
fast for me. Do not eat or drink for three days, night or
day. I and my maids will fast as you do. When this is

done, I will go to the king, even though it is against the law. And if I perish, I perish."
—Esther 4:16

Three days later, Esther dressed in her royal gown and went to King Xerxes' courtyard. When the king saw Esther, he held out his golden scepter, an action that allowed her to come into his presence.

Then the king asked, "What is it, Queen Esther? What is your request? Even up to half the kingdom, it will be given to you."

"If it pleases the king," replied Esther, "let the king, together with Haman, come today to a banquet I have prepared for him."
—Esther 5:3–4

During dinner that evening the king asked Esther what her request was. She answered by inviting the king and Haman to a second banquet the following evening.

Prideful Haman went home to boast to his wife and friends how he had attended Queen Esther's banquet with the king. He also spoke of his intense hatred for Mordecai. That evening he ordered a gallows to be built on which he intended to hang Mordecai.

At the queen's banquet the next evening King Xerxes again asked Esther for her petition. She replied:

"Grant me my life—this is my petition. And spare my people—this is my request. For I and my people have been sold for destruction and slaughter and annihilation." . . .

"King Xerxes asked Queen Esther, "Who is he? Where is the man who has dared to do such a thing?"

Esther said, "The adversary and enemy is this vile Haman."
—Esther 7:3, 5, 6

Haman's folly caught up with him. King Xerxes ordered that Haman be hanged on the gallows he'd built for Mordecai.

Esther's faith and courage saved her people, and her cousin Mordecai was given the king's signet ring. The Jews celebrated with a day of feasting and joy. Today Jews still celebrate Purim in remembrance of God's deliverance.

Lessons we learn from Esther:

- Make decisions wisely.
- Stand firm in the face of injustice.
- Step out in faith.
- Confront the abuser with well-made plans.

Reflections

If you're still working on believing in yourself, what do you need to do next?

Lord, help me to believe that through Your guidance I am a person worthy of love.

CHAPTER 10

Setting Boundaries

*Consider it pure joy, my brothers, whenever you face trials of
many kinds, because you know that the testing of your faith
develops perseverance. Perseverance must finish its work so
that you may be mature and complete, not lacking anything.*
—James 1:2–4

We often hear the phrase "Life is a balancing act." This
may conjure up images of a clown juggling balls or a
monkey such as Curious George balancing an enormous stack
of hats on his head. These are whimsical examples that bring
a smile to our lips.

Yet there is a more serious connotation to the phrase "Life
is a balancing act." For instance, living with emotional and
verbal abuse is like trying to keep our balance on a tightrope
while suffering from vertigo. To regain our balance, we must
step down from the tightrope onto safe ground.

Boundaries indicate limits—lines not to be crossed. To
acquire mental or emotional stability and overcome the
trauma of verbal abuse, an individual needs to put boundaries
in place. It may seem impossible at first, even awkward,
to implement the use of emotional boundaries in a relationship.
Like juggling clowns, we may sometimes drop the balls
that represent our convictions: belief in ourselves, courage,
and renewed hope. To become a proficient juggler takes
practice. If we drop the balls, we need to pick them up and
start over.

Walking away from an abuser during a rampage or stating, "It's not OK for you to talk to me in that manner" are actions that draw invisible boundaries.

IN THE FOLLOWING STORY we meet a woman named Sarah who never learned about boundaries. As a result her adult children and other family members took advantage.

Carrying a Balanced Load
Dr. Mary M. Simms

"Can you help me feel better today, Doc? I'm so tired. I can't sleep or concentrate, so it's difficult to go to work every day."

"It sounds like you are depressed, Sarah," I replied. "Let's get some additional history on you. What do you do for a living?"

She answered sheepishly, "Oh, I'm a caregiver. I take care of sick people."

"How many days a week do you work?" I asked.

"Well," she said, "I work six days a week."

"Do you have to work six days? Is that a requirement of the job?

"The person I work for needs me," Sarah answered defensively. "The weekend caregiver quit, so I am the only person who is available."

I interjected, "It sounds like you are making your employer's problem your problem."

"Well, I want to be a loyal and faithful person. That is what God wants. Isn't it?

"And what is your family life like?" I asked.

"My two adult children came back to live with me because they were laid off. It was supposed to be a temporary situation until they got on their feet, but it has turned into five years for Connie and three years for Jim. They don't seem to be trying to help themselves."

"Are they paying you rent?"

"No. I thought if they didn't pay anything that they could save up and purchase their own homes. Now, Connie has quit her job and decided that she needs to find herself—whatever that means. My husband got laid off his job, as well. He just can't seem to find and keep a good job."

"No wonder you are tired," I commented. "You are busy taking care of a lot of adults."

"Well, you know, God tells us that we are supposed to help one another, so I'm really trying my best to do His will."

"So, did you help a lot of people when you were growing up?"

"Yes, my mom divorced my dad when I was five years old. I remember learning how to fry chicken when I was six."

"You were expected to fry chicken at six years old!" I responded in shocked amazement.

"Yes, Mom used to scold me when I failed at cooking the meat thoroughly. Also, being the oldest child, I helped take care of my younger sister and brother."

"Were you much older?" I asked.

"Well, let me think . . . I am five years older than Louise, and three years older than Ellis."

"What were your responsibilities with your siblings?"

"Well, because Mom worked a lot, I had the responsibility of cooking dinner and making sure the house was in order when she came home. I also made sure that Louise and Ellis did their homework and house chores. If one of them got in trouble, I got yelled at for not doing my job! To this day they still look up to me," she stated proudly. "They are always asking me for money and suggestions on what to do about certain situations."

"Who told you that you were responsible for Louise and Ellis?

"Oh," she answered, "I know that as an adult I'm not responsible for them anymore. However, I can still hear Mom's voice in my head screaming, 'You are responsible because you're the oldest!' It's funny, now that I think about it, I often hear my husband scream the same thing in a different way."

"What do you mean, 'in a different way?'"

"He often tells me that I should be ashamed of myself for making him feel guilty about not finding a job. He says he is doing the best he can. And you know, maybe he is. He has had some difficult times in his life, and I guess I should be more patient."

● ● ●

Growing up, Sarah did not learn where her responsibilities began and where they ended. This blurred understanding continued to affect her ability to value herself and live a balanced life.

These vague boundaries continued through adulthood because of the beliefs that are tied to them: "You are responsible because you are the oldest." "You were born to take care of others—put yourself last." "You should feel badly when the people you are responsible for don't do well."

The guilt from these messages played over and over in Sarah's head. Then in life's circumstances that guilt became overwhelming and led to depression and an inability to feel free. Additionally, her distorted view about what it means to be a Christian also contributed to reinforced guilt and distorted thinking in this area. Sarah used her faith to justify her need to take on more than she could adequately handle.

People with such a background could take Scripture verses such as Galatians 6:2—"*Carry each other's burdens, and in this way you will fulfill the law of Christ*"—to justify their distorted belief that they should continue to hurt themselves by financially or emotionally carrying others. God desires for us to be good stewards of the resources He gives us, and He tells us to walk with wisdom in the use of our time, resources, and gifts.

One interpretation of this Scripture is that we ought to have compassion for one another, practicing empathy. We are commanded as Christians, disciples of Christ, to love and help one another. However, farther down, Galatians 6:5 reads, *"for each one should carry his own load."* In other words, all persons must answer to God for themselves. We also need to realize that keeping a balance between helping others and taking care of ourselves is a juggling act.

Saboteur
Connie L. Peters

There arose in my life an enemy
Who threw obstacles in my way.
Just when victory was nearly mine
Defeat moved in to stay.

Who is this saboteur
Who brings my plans to naught?
I asked the Lord to intervene
That this villain would be caught.

I asked Him to defeat this foe
And grant me eyes to see.
He did, and to my surprise,
I found the foe was me.

Fear of success? How can this be?
Isn't victory what we all choose?
But He looked down deep and showed me
If I thought I'd won, I'd lose.

Help me overcome this fear
And accept what you have in store.

You know what is good for me,
And you want to bless me more.

AFTER MANY YEARS of destructive behavior, Kimberly Davidson
learned how to set boundaries with her dad and how to say no.

Exercising the "No" Muscle
Kimberly Davidson

"Get on the scale! I bet you weigh 140 pounds!" He dared me
over and over to weigh myself. He snatched the plate of food
away as I reached for seconds. "You can't have that—you're
fat!" The humiliation was overwhelming. *If my dad thinks I'm
fat, then everyone else must think so, too.*

What started as a diet at age 18 ended up being a 20-year
battle with the eating disorder, bulimia, as well as other self-
destructive behaviors. I felt determined to stay thin at any
cost. That meant abusing substances like alcohol, cigarettes,
diet pills, diuretics, and laxatives. I became obsessed with my
body image. I thought, *If I am thinner and prettier, life will be
perfect. I'll be a success, and Dad will be proud of me.*

As I grew up, I learned to conform to the way I thought
my dad, and the world, wanted me to be. I was addicted to
approval. Why? Because I feared rejection—like the kind I had
received from my dad. I lost 15 pounds. My dad commended
me, "You look terrific! Good job!" Yet I craved more praise.

As the years passed, I realized that bulimia was a monster that wanted to eat me alive. Ashamed, I refused to ask
anyone for help, especially my dad. I didn't dare disappoint
him again. So I tried to heal myself by reading self-help books
until I thought my head would explode, but nothing worked.
The lies. The secrecy. The shame. *I can't take living this way
anymore!* I cried, *Help!*

Wounded by Words

Then I met Jesus Christ, and He slowly began to pull me out of my battlefield—the bathroom. I discovered God wanted control over my life. I struggled with that and thought, *I'm used to being in control. No, that's not true. My addiction has made life unmanageable. It controls me.*

Over time I surrendered my heart and soul to God. Together we started on an incredible journey to clean up the emotional garbage that led to my addictions. Like an onion, my heart and soul were wrapped with layers of hurts. I had to allow God to peel away each layer to do His work in me.

In order to grow I had to release the hurts of my past. This included forgiving Dad for the destructive things he'd said. By surrendering all my hurt feelings of rejection to God, I began to heal. Then He could help me forgive those who had hurt and rejected me.

I recovered from my addiction. Then for the first time in my life I learned to create boundaries.

Doing so consisted of several steps:

1. I had to carve out my own identity. Through Scripture I defined who I was. Genesis 1:27 says, *"God created human beings in his own image"* (NLT). Ephesians 2:10 says, *"For we are God's workmanship, created in Christ Jesus to do good works, which God prepared in advance for us to do."* I realized that this is who I am. I am more than a body!

2. I defined who I was *not*. I started to express my feelings and make personal choices. I began to accept my dad just as he was because God tells us to love one another and not judge.

3. I started to work out a new muscle—the "no" muscle. "No" had been eliminated from my vocabulary. I stopped acting as an enabler, especially to the men in my life. I had allowed them to take advantage of me, to be self-centered and irresponsible like my dad. I began to set limits.

For example, a situation arose where my dad told my husband and me exactly what we should do in regard to selling our car. Dad sent several detailed emails, which basically said, "You're too dumb to figure this out. I don't trust you to do this on your own—so do what I say." The old Kim would have buckled and followed each line item to a T because she believed the lies. After discussing the situation with God through prayer, I explained rationally and politely to my dad why his advice would *not* work. The lion retreated back into his den. Boundaries work!

I replaced distorted thinking (lies) with the truth. For decades I believed in false ideals and cultural lies like *I am unlovable and unworthy. I am fat and ugly and always will be. I'm a loser.*

I participated in Bible studies and learned new truths like this one: *"I can do everything through him who gives me strength"* (Philippians 4:13).

I also realized that God will help me make wise decisions if I ask Him: *"If any of you lacks wisdom, he should ask God, who gives generously to all without finding fault, and it will be given to him"* (James 1:5). My self-esteem increased when I let go of distorted stereotypes and began responding to God's Word.

God restored my spiritual, physical, emotional, and relational nature, and I became the person God created me to be. Today I am 50 years old, and my father still attempts to control my life. He hasn't changed, but I have. Today when my dad says something demanding or demeaning, I take my hurts to God and ask Him to handle the situation. And through His special touch, somehow the love is restored between my dad and me.

● ● ●

Accepting Christ is paramount, but acceptance requires change, and we are the only ones who can implement that change, as did Kimberly. She decided no longer to live under the domination, control, and futility of trying to please her father.

Jeenie experienced a similar circumstance with her former husband. "So you think this house is clean!" he screamed, as he ran his fingers over the top of the door jam and extracted some dust.

"No matter how much I tried, I always failed. He needed to blame me in order to justify his lifestyle," said Jeenie.

We will never become whole until we get out from under the narcissistic jurisdiction of another and find our own way through God's help.

ALTHOUGH THE VERBAL ABUSE escalated to physical, Carol learned to set boundaries. With prayer and counseling, her marriage was saved.

Out of Control
Carol Davis

Every time a nurse entered my hospital room I wanted to hide. I felt so ashamed. My bruised body didn't matter, but the man I looked to for protection and love had put me there, and that did matter.

"I hate him. Do you hear me, Lord? I hate Mark for beating me and putting me in this hospital bed."

Mark had never hit me before our lives took a dramatic turn. Our son was run over by a car and died. We lost our business to bankruptcy, and my father dropped dead of a heart attack. All this happened within a three-month period, and that's when Mark started physically abusing me. When I was hospitalized and Mark got caught, he looked scared. Yet, when I left the hospital, I went home with him.

The physical side of abuse stopped, but not the verbal. Strange, but I never thought of his demeaning words as abusive. Perhaps it's because I believed what he said. I felt unworthy. Losing my son added to my low self-esteem, because moms aren't supposed to let their children die. I didn't know that the loss of a child often causes marital problems.

Then one day I realized I couldn't take it anymore. I fought back physically by throwing a crystal vase at Mark's head, but it hit a closed window, shattering glass everywhere. I didn't stop there, I threw a plant, and it hit the living room wall. Then I tossed a hot broiler onto the kitchen floor, burning a hole in it.

Mark just stood there in shock. He turned away and cried out, "You're ruining my house."

His house!

"I want to save our marriage, Carol. But you act like you don't care." Then he walked away.

"Lord, I don't know how to fight back. We are headed for divorce." I felt numb and could hardly believe Mark wanted to save our marriage.

I don't want to be married. I just want peace. "Mark, I want you to leave our home," I said, but I was surprised when he actually left.

A short time later a sympathetic girlfriend consoled me. "Carol, read this book. I think you're in a verbally abusive relationship."

"OK," I said. But I thought, *Mark is just better with words.*

When I read the book, it took my breath away. It described my husband's actions. I realized, *He is a verbal abuser.* The book gave examples of controlling relationships.

My husband's words did control me. Often he had asked, "Why do you take everything so seriously? I was just joking."

Later in a phone conversation with Mark, I found the courage to talk to my husband about what I'd learned. "Mark, I read this book, and I want you to read it, too. It's about verbal abuse. It describes what we are going through."

"Carol, if I'm verbally abusing you, it's your fault."

"No, Mark, it's not my fault. If you're not willing to read this book and to get help, our 20-year marriage will end in divorce."

When I said those words, my heart felt like it was breaking. To stand up against abuse is never easy, but at that point I didn't care.

"Mark, I understand that you are hurting inside. The abuse is a result of your pain."

Then a therapist who belonged to our church told us we needed to join a class if we wanted to save our marriage.

We agreed to attend a series called "Learning to Live, Learning to Love." The course taught me how to recognize abuse and the causes that fuel the abuser. We had to go every week for an entire year. The classes were not only a serious commitment, but they were also expensive.

As a couple we learned to communicate and to "fight fair." We learned that whenever a hurtful word was spoken, we needed to sit down immediately and talk it out, which we did. We never let one little word slip by even if we thought, *Oh, that's not worth making a big deal over.* But it was! Not even one little word can slip by because it will fester and eat away like a cancer that grows until it smothers your spirit. It's like an alcoholic saying, "One little drink won't matter."

Today, our love and marriage remain strong. We overcame abuse by recognizing it, getting professional help, confronting it, and talking it out.

The tendency to abuse will always be there with my husband, but just like living with an alcoholic, you have to weigh your ability to confront and overcome this terrible demon. Through the grace of God, we were able to do this.

● ● ●

"Standing over the casket of my nine-year-old nephew and gazing into his little face, my heart ached," Jeenie lamented. "Watching the gut-wrenching pain of his parents broke my heart."

Many marriages do not survive after parents lose a child because they tend to grieve alone, excluding their mate. Thus, they grow further and further apart, and eventually the marriage disintegrates. Most of the couples Jeenie has seen in therapy who have lost a child have been unable to reunite. They chose divorce as their option.

Even though the death of their child was horrific, Mark and Carol were able to build a wholesome marriage. Theirs is truly a victorious story.

"GIFTS, PARTIES, AND CARDS seemed satisfying ways to end a teaching career that spanned 43 years. Instead, I faced a crisis that blistered my spirit and left me groping for answers," states Evelyn. This teacher faced circumstances that required her to take drastic steps to protect herself from a student who was out of control.

Taking a Stand
S. Evelyn Evans

The first week Isaac, a 16-year-old student, entered my class he created a disturbance. He made graphic comments about his mother's recent honeymoon. The next week, he taunted other students. That's when the counselor and principal took action, but Isaac didn't respond.

In the spring, Isaac exploded in class, and I asked him to leave. He cursed and stormed out. This time I asked for a meeting with Isaac's father to work out a behavioral plan.

Isaac was placed in detention the next day, but he decided he wouldn't go. I stopped him when he came to the classroom and walked with him toward the principal's office. Isaac walked behind me, muttering words I couldn't distinguish. When we reached the office, I opened the door and motioned for Isaac to enter. He hesitated, glared at me, and then spoke to a student, who was seated in the office. "I'm going to have to kill that ol' hag."

The other student jumped up and ran out to spread the news, "Isaac says he's going to kill Mrs. Evans."

Within the hour, students buzzed and teachers came to ask what had happened. The principal called Isaac's father, who came to school. I expected we could work together to get help for Isaac, but this wasn't to be. The father said, "Isaac had been in trouble at other schools. I guess we'll have to move again."

That meant Isaac would not get the help he needed.

The next morning the police officer called to ask, "'Do you want to press charges?"

This was not a small question, for it involved not only Isaac and his family but teachers and students. At first, like many other victims of verbal threats, I blamed myself. Maybe I could have handled the situation differently. Maybe there was some other way to insulate the school from violence. Then I thought of recent school shootings, which had consumed the evening news. Teachers and students had ignored threats until libraries and classrooms were washed with the blood of the innocent. My life's work had been nurturing students, and I had grandchildren in schools. I wanted to do my part in protecting all of them both from harm.

I decided I had no other recourse. When angry words and disagreements turn to violent threats, people must protect themselves and others through legal means. Sadly, I answered, "I want students to feel safe at school. I'll press charges."

The police officer got an arrest warrant that day, but Isaac did not go home. Four days later, when he was still free, I feared he might be stalking me.

The officer had advised me not to return to school, so I sat home alone. I stared into space, unable to focus and move ahead. In need of comfort, I turned to Scripture:

Since my youth, O God, you have taught me,
and to this day I declare your marvelous deeds.
Even when I am old and gray, do not forsake me,

O God, till I declare your power to the next generation,
your might to all who are to come.
                    —Psalms 71:17–18

Later that day Isaac was arrested, and the juvenile court assigned a probation officer. Fearing this would not be good for Isaac, I called my state and professional teachers' groups only to learn they consult with schools and not individuals. My church and school friends didn't know how to deal with terrorist threats. I found no lawyers who had handled terrorist threats. A teacher friend advised me to drop the case, but I felt Isaac couldn't successfully navigate life as a bully. He needed to learn to control his speech.

Since the age of seven, God had been my Rock, and now I called upon Him. I also continued to rely upon Scripture and my family. The next week, I went back to work even though my fear had been compounded by another death threat. In response to this alarm, the administration asked all teachers to lock classroom doors before each period. This provided some protection for the rest of the school year.

Four months after the threat, the prosecuting attorney called about a possible court date. I learned there had been a full investigation, and the prosecution would proceed if I was ready to testify. I assured them I would be there, and the case was scheduled for trial.

The day of the trial, my husband and church friends came to pray. One of my friends, who knew Isaac's father, approached him before the trial to say she had prayed for Isaac. He brushed aside her concern by justifying his son's actions.

Waiting to testify, I felt like a pat of butter on a hot griddle. On the stand, though, I felt God's presence as the prosecutors skillfully handled the questioning and closing remarks. When Isaac took the witness stand he said, "The threat was just a prank."

It took the jury only one and one-half hours to find Isaac guilty of a terrorist threat. Three persons on the jury returned to offer words of support and to hear the court mandate an alternative school and counseling for Isaac.

Isaac completed a semester of alternative school and left town. In time, a security fence was built around my old school. And I recognized that the storms of life are resolved by waiting and trusting God, who gave me the gift of faith so I could look beyond the unwelcome preretirement events. I still pray that Isaac will someday be changed by the concern of his teachers and the power of God's grace.

● ● ●

The seeds of kindness and wisdom Evelyn sowed in Isaac's life will hopefully pay off someday. In counseling hundreds of incarcerated young men (some murderers), Jeenie often told them, "I don't care whether you remember my name, but hopefully the things I've said and prayed for you will bring change to your life." God is responsible for the outcome—not us. Our job is to be faithful to Him.

An excellent example of faith in the face of adversity is the story of Joseph. Stripped of his dignity, his home, and his identity, Joseph realized life as he'd known it had ended. After being sold to a caravan of Ishmaelites, Joseph was carried farther and farther into the wilderness. While he endured sweltering heat, sleepless nights, and broken dreams, he must have thought, *My own brothers have done this evil thing—sold me into slavery.*

Meanwhile another drama unfolded, as Jacob, his father, clutched Joseph's cloak of many colors, his tears mingling with the blood. *"It is my son's robe! Some ferocious animal has devoured him. Joseph has surely been torn to pieces"* (Genesis 37:33).

How could Jacob know that the ferocious animal was Joseph's own brothers, driven by a green-eyed monster called jealousy? The final straw had been Joseph's youthful boasting about a dream he'd had—a dream where his brothers and father bowed down to him. His brothers' rage over the dream had led to a vicious plot, deceitful lies, and irrevocable actions.

In Egypt, Joseph was purchased from the Ishmaelites by Potiphar, captain of Pharaoh's guard. The Lord blessed the house of the Egyptian because of Joseph. Potiphar left Joseph in charge of his entire household. For a long time things went well until...

Now Joseph was well-built and handsome, and after a while his master's wife took notice of Joseph and said, "Come to bed with me . . ."

"My Master has withheld nothing from me except you, because you are his wife. How then could I do such a wicked thing and sin against God?"

—Genesis 39:6–9

Potiphar's wife did not want to take no for an answer. It is safe to say she stalked him on a daily basis, only to be turned down time after time.

Joseph set his boundaries firmly in place while Potiphar's wife waited like a lioness, watching for the right moment to entrap her prey. Then one day when all her servants were away, Joseph appeared. She attacked, sinking in her claws of deception. *"She caught him by his cloak and said, 'Come to bed with me!' But he left his cloak in her hand and ran out of the house"* (Genesis 39:12).

Potiphar's wife played the role of the typical abuser, pointing a finger of blame at Joseph. She declared to her servants and finally to her husband that Joseph had tried to seduce her. She claimed he ran when she screamed. Potiphar burned with anger against Joseph and had him sent to prison.

While in prison Joseph's reputation for interpreting dreams eventually reached the Pharaoh of Egypt. He sent for Joseph when no one could interpret a dream he'd had.

Joseph predicted that Pharaoh's dream told of seven plentiful years in Egypt and then seven years of famine. Even Pharaoh realized that God's spirit blessed Joseph, and he promoted him to second in power over all of Egypt. Joseph prepared Egypt for the lean times.

Meanwhile, famine was spreading worldwide. Jacob's family began to suffer, and Jacob sent ten of his sons to Egypt to buy grain. Face-to-face with the brother they had sold into slavery, they did not recognize Joseph. He tested them and asked questions about their family. Then he accused them of being spies and placed them in jail for three days.

Since Joseph used an interpreter, they did not know he understood them.

They said to one another, "Surely we are being punished because of our brother. We saw how distressed he was when he pleaded with us for his life, but we would not listen; that's why this distress has come upon us."
—Genesis 42:21

Scripture records five times that Joseph wept. We can only imagine how the pain in Joseph's heart must have grieved him. Eventually he revealed to his brothers the truth—that the brother sold into slavery and the man second in control of all Egypt were one and the same. How Joseph's brothers must have trembled at the news! Surely he'd punish them!

But Joseph had no plans for revenge. Instead he forgave them. In time, Jacob and his household moved to Egypt near Joseph and were able to escape the famine.

We read in Genesis 48:11 Jacob's touching words toward Joseph's sons born to an Egyptian mother. *"I never expected to see your face again, and now God has allowed me to see your children too."*

Lessons we learn from Joseph:
- He did not give in to the demands of a controlling person.
- He did not seek revenge.
- He maintained a good attitude.
- He expressed his feelings.
- He remained faithful to God and himself.

Reflections

Describe how setting boundaries has made a difference in your life.

Lord, help me to know
what boundaries to set.

CHAPTER 11

Liking the New Me

Fear not, for I have redeemed you; I have summoned you by name; you are mine.

When you pass through the waters, I will be with you; and when you pass through the rivers, they will not sweep over you.

When you walk through the fire, you will not be burned; the flames will not set you ablaze.

For I am the LORD, your God, the Holy One of Israel, your Savior.

—Isaiah 43:1–3

No one deserves to be emotionally abused—even an ugly duckling. Hans Christian Andersen tells a delightful story about an enormous ugly duckling who was teased and tormented. Other ducks in the barnyard made comments like, "What a dreadful-looking creature that duckling is"; "In time I expect his looks will improve or his size won't be so noticeable"; and "He was in the egg too long, that's why he isn't properly shaped." The ducks bit him, the hens pecked him, and the girl who fed them kicked him with her foot. So the ugly duckling ran away, but even wild ducks said, "You are appallingly ugly." He was berated so long that he came to believe that he truly was ugly.

Then in the spring he flew into a beautiful garden where he saw some magnificent swans. He said, "I will fly near those royal birds, and they will peck me to death for daring to bring my ugly self near them."

Yet when he swam near them, he happened to look down into the water at his own reflection. To his surprise, he realized that he was no longer an awkward, dirty gray bird. He himself was a magnificent swan.

The storyteller comments, "He felt quite glad to have been through so much trouble and adversity, for now he could fully appreciate not only his own good fortune, but also all the beauty that greeted him."

Andersen concludes this delightful tale with the swan saying, "I never dreamt that so much happiness was possible when I was the ugly duckling."

Like the ugly duckling, we may have been mistreated by others. Yet, we, too, need to develop a new attitude toward ourselves. We need to learn to treat ourselves with respect and to like ourselves. If we allow ourselves to make new friends and to try new things, in time our confidence will build, opening up new opportunities for us. After all, in God's eyes we are all magnificent swans.

IT TOOK 11 YEARS for Barbara to realize that in God's eyes she was not ugly, but a person wonderfully made in God's image.

My Time to Shine
Barbara Oden

"I don't love you anymore, and I don't know if I ever did." My husband's words cut me to the core, and in a flash he walked out. With my three-year-old son in my arms, I stood in my living room dazed. Everything I believed to be true about my life fell apart in the span of time it took my husband to spew out those caustic words.

Ten years later, the destructive words still influenced every facet of my life. I had allowed someone else's words to define me, and I lost myself along the way. Like a rope around my neck, the words choked the life from me and destroyed my self-esteem.

Decision time: I could continue to live like a victim or let go and walk as a victor. I chose to walk in victory. Within a matter of days, I contacted a Christian counselor and began the long road to recovery.

In counseling I discovered I had not only put myself in the path of hurtful words at home, but I had allowed the same kind of verbal abuse at work. Caustic, untrue words were bleeding into every aspect of my life.

"You know you have a child to raise alone and no time to go back to college. You are better off staying in this job where I can help you. Barbara, you would not survive in another department in this company. You won't get a better opportunity anywhere else," my supervisor said on more than one occasion.

His constant putdowns seeped into me like a deadly poison. His criticisms exploited my single-parent status to create insecurity and fear within me. His condescending words seemed to erase in my mind the excellent job ratings I received from peers and other managers.

My ex-husband proved how unlovable I am, so my supervisor must be right, too, I thought. It never occurred to me that in order to gain respect, I had to first respect myself. I tore myself down with the very words I'd heard from others. How does a person learn to respect herself after feeling worthless for so long?

By the time I started my counseling journey, I had been divorced for 11 years and in my then-present job for 8. My counselor began unraveling the untruths spoken by my ex-husband. She also showed me how I had allowed those untruths to spill over into my job and other relationships.

Undoing the harm demeaning words had carved on my soul became one of the most difficult challenges I ever faced. Counseling took time, patience, and a lot of gut-wrenching honesty. I relived many painful events in order to put them into perspective. I learned to respect myself again and appreciate who I am in Christ. I felt brand new. Seeing the past more clearly set me free! I could finally begin to believe what God saw in me the day He created me.

Breaking free from untruths led me back to all the possibilities God had planned for my life. I learned to dream again and to see those dreams become reality.

God showed me through His Word who I am in Christ:
- I am not condemned (Romans 8:1).
- I am accepted (Romans 15:7).
- I am chosen (Ephesians 1:4).
- I am forgiven (Ephesians 1:7).
- I am wonderfully made (Psalm 139:14).

Praise God, I finally reached a place to allow Him to renew my belief in myself!

Six months into counseling, I felt strong and ready to move—literally! I took a huge leap and applied for a high-profile position in my company. Within one week, news of my promotion arrived. I felt excited to have a fresh start with new people. It was my time to shine!

Today, I believe in myself and even like the new me. When doubt creeps back in and I feel overwhelmed, I remember who God says I am. God's positive talk about me demonstrates the magnitude of His love for me. I know His love—not the negative words of others—defines me.

● ● ●

How sad that Barbara took 11 years to get much needed counseling. She suffered needlessly. But how inspiring it is that she found the freedom to see herself as a person created in God's beautiful image

> "So God created man in his own image, in the image of God he created him; male and female he created them."
> —Genesis 1:27

Here is an illustration Jeenie often uses at speaking engagements as well as in therapy: "Picture me in the deep end of the pool with a gigantic multicolored beach ball. It is very important to me that no one knows I have the ball, so I shove it under the water and sit on it. I must keep a close eye on the ball and move when it does, so it remains submerged. Even though I can smile and wave, my energy is concentrated on keeping the ball below the surface. One hand is always ready to push it down, should it begin to pop up.

"Instead, suppose I decide to stop hiding the ball. Now, I can run around the pool, eat, talk to people, swim—whatever I choose. I'm free."

Such is the case with people who desperately try to keep their pain submerged (repressed). Much of their energy is wasted on pretending. When they choose to "let up the ball" (deal with their feelings), only then will they become truly free. They can delegate the painful memories to the past—forever.

CONNIE SHARES A POEM based on her childhood:

The Muffler Dragon
Connie L. Peters

One cold, dark night our family of seven
were stuffed into the station wagon.
We heard a roar, and Dad proclaimed,
"It's the Muffler Dragon!"

Fear gripped my six-year-old heart,
but soon I felt like braggin'.
With just a wire, my own brave dad
defeated the Muffler Dragon.

I pictured it by the roadside,
crying, its head waggin'.
And I almost pitied
that mean ol' Muffler Dragon
Through the years, I faced my fears
when my feelings were laggin'.
I realized that my greatest terror
had been just the muffler draggin'.

So, at times, when you feel
your own emotions saggin',
search your mind, for you may find
it was only a Muffler Dragon.

"FEEL THE DIGNITY of a child. Do not feel superior to him, for you are not." This quote by Robert Henri, a famous painter, expresses the importance of respecting the dignity of a small child like Connie Lee. Simple things can have damaging effects on our lives, as Connie's story shows.

"My Name's Not Connie Marie!"
Connie L. Peters

One Muffler Dragon I had to deal with occurred when my great uncle used to call me Connie Marie. At the tender age of three it infuriated me. My middle name is Lee. I used to stamp my foot and shout, "My name's not Connie Marie!" And, of course, others joined in on my uncle's teasing and called me Connie Marie just to see me have a fit.

As a result, feeling like no one understands me, knows me, or even sees me is something I have dealt with all my life.

Years later, God spoke to me as I read the story of Hagar in Genesis 16. When Hagar, pregnant with Ishmael, fled Sarai, an angel spoke to her and told her to go back and submit to Sarai. God promised that Ishmael's descendants would become a great nation.

"She gave this name to the LORD who spoke to her: 'You are the God who sees me,' for she said, 'I have now seen the One who sees me'" (Genesis 16:13).

As I read this Scripture the Holy Spirit impressed on my heart: "I love you; I see you; and I know your name is Connie Lee." It reminded me to base my understanding of who I am on what God says, not what others think about me—nor on my Muffler Dragons. Our healing from verbal abuse begins when we see the God who sees us.

● ● ●

"'IT'S NOT THE SIZE of the man in the fight, but the size of the fight in the man!' my dad often said. Since he was no giant himself, I figured he knew what he was talking about. Still, no amount of fight could overcome my lack of size." Although Peggy Rose's dad always tried to encourage her, she didn't learn how to accept herself until God showed her how He valued her inner beauty.

How Others See Me
Peggy Matthews Rose

"Well," said the personnel interviewer, "I can offer you something in a couple of departments, but I'm afraid you're not tall enough for most of our jobs here."

Because I'd married a co-worker, I had to choose—either leave the company or find another area to work in. I didn't want to leave the entertainment job I loved so much, but rules were rules, and the company did not allow married couples to work in the same department. Neither of the options offered thrilled my dreamer's soul. Still, I faced the facts and chose the first department with an opening.

In 1970, suing for discrimination had not yet been invented. Besides, I knew he was right. Every other role in this outdoor entertainment venue required being seen over the crowds. At less than five feet tall, I might have gotten attention in a crowd of hobbits, but everywhere else I was passed over. I appeared invisible.

As it turned out, the "lesser of two evil jobs" worked out, and I stayed for five years. But the sting of those words, "You're not tall enough," gave me a complex. It was bad enough they were true! The interviewer didn't have to rub it in. It's not as if I didn't know I was short! As a kid, I'd been the tallest in class, the first one chosen for basketball and volleyball teams. Then somewhere on the road to junior high, my growth came to a screeching halt.

"Good things come in small packages!" Boy, was I tired of hearing *that* line. When I'd worked in a counter-service food establishment, I heard, "Hey, you standin' in a hole back there?" Why did these people always think they were funny?

Finally an opportunity came my way to intern in a management position. The training department needed writers to create training handbooks. With my English literature degree, I walked into the interview and presented myself as the person they needed. Fortunately for me, they agreed. They didn't care about my height. That internship eventually turned into a position writing for the company newsletter and later serving as editor.

I have many fond memories of that position. My favorite is the day I sat, newly hired, working at the drawing board when in walked the department manager—the same interviewer who had told me years earlier I was "too short" for any other job. Surprised to see me, he tried to hide it with a pleasant greeting. But at that moment, it sure felt good to say to him, "Bet you didn't know short people can write!" Fortunately for me, he laughed.

Wounded by Words

It would be a few more years before I had a life-changing encounter with Jesus Christ. It took Him to show me the truth about myself—that I'd been shaped by the Potter's hands, and He'd made me to please Himself, a container to hold His truth. Who was I to complain? What a difference that truth made in my life! No more bitterness at being overlooked for prom queen, tour guide, or attraction hostess. And today I continue to write, hoping my words will bring glory to God.

● ◉ ●

Jeenie says, "I, too, am one of the small people of the world and have heard similar comments. Over the years, however, I have learned to accept myself and, for the most part, view my height in the normal range. Often after I leave a speaking platform and interact, people comment, 'Wow, I didn't know you were so small.' In my stage demeanor and presentation, my message comes across—not my stature."

Everyone has one imperfection or another to deal with in life. If we choose to focus on it, others will follow our lead. Conversely, if it does not matter much to us, we will come through unscathed.

> *Do not let any unwholesome talk come out of your mouths,*
> *but only what is helpful for building others up according to*
> *their needs, that it may benefit those who listen.*
> —Ephesians 4:29

NANCY LEARNED THE WISDOM of that verse in the following story.

The Parable of the Coffee Filter
Nancy C. Anderson

My brother Dan said, "I'm going home! Your bickering is making me crazy. You two fight constantly—and it wears me out."

I defended our behavior. "Hey, it's not like we disagree about *everything*. Ron and I agree on all the major issues. We hardly ever fight about 'big stuff' like where to go to church, how to raise Nick, or who's a better driver—me. We just disagree about the 'little stuff.'"

He sighed and said, "Well, I'm sick of hearing you go to war over where to put the towel rack, which TV shows to watch, or who did—or didn't—use a coaster. It's all dumb stuff. None of it will matter a year from now. I can tell that Ron is really mad by the way he *stomped* up the stairs. Why did you have to criticize the way he mowed the lawn? I know it wasn't perfect, but couldn't you just let it go?"

"No," I replied, "We are having company tomorrow, and I want the yard to be perfect. So I told him to fix it—big deal! Anyway, I won, because he removed it."

Dan shook his head. "If you keep this up, you may win the arguments, but lose your husband."

I slugged his arm. "Oh, stop being so melodramatic!"

The next evening, Ron and I went out to dinner with some friends we hadn't seen in several years. We remembered George as being funny and outgoing, but he seemed rather quiet, and he looked exhausted. His wife, Beth, did most of the talking. She told us about her fabulous accomplishments and then endlessly bragged about her brilliant, Mensa-bound children. She only mentioned George to criticize him.

After we ordered our dinner, she said, "George, I saw you flirting with that waitress!" (He wasn't.)

"George," she whined, "can't you do anything right? You are holding your fork like a little kid!" (He was.)

When he mispronounced an item on the dessert menu, she said, "No wonder you flunked out of college, you can't read!" She laughed so hard that she snorted, but she was the only one laughing.

George didn't respond. He just looked at us with an empty face and a blank stare. Then he shrugged his sad shoulders. The rest of the evening was oppressive as she continued to harangue and harass him about almost everything he said or did. I thought, *I wonder if this is how my brother feels when I criticize Ron.*

We said good-bye to Beth and George and left the restaurant in silence. When we got in the car, I spoke first. "Do I sound like her?"

"You're not *that* bad."

"How bad am I?"

"Pretty bad," Ron half whispered.

The next morning, as I poured water into the coffeepot, I looked over at my "Devotions for Wives" calendar. I read: "The wise woman builds her house, but with her own hands the foolish one tears hers down." *Or with her own mouth*, I thought.

"A quarrelsome wife is as annoying as constant dripping on a rainy day." *How can I stop this horrible pattern?*

"Take control of what I say, O Lord, and guard my lips. Don't let me drift toward evil." *O Lord, show me how!*

I carefully spooned the vanilla-nut decaf into the pot, as I remembered the day I forgot the filter. The coffee was bitter and full of undrinkable grounds. I had to throw it away. I thought, *The coffee, without filtering, is like my coarse and bitter speech.*

I prayed, "Oh, please Lord, install a filter between my brain and my mouth. Help me to choose my words carefully and let my speech be smooth and mellow. Thank you for teaching me the parable of the coffee filter. I won't forget it."

An hour later, Ron timidly asked, "What do you think about moving the couch over by the window? We'll be able to see the TV better."

My first thought was to tell him why that was a dumb idea. *The couch will fade if you put it in the sunlight, and besides, you already watch too much TV.* But, instead of my usual hasty reply, I let the coarse thoughts drip through my newly installed filter and calmly said, "That might be a good idea. Let's try it for a few days and see if we like it. I'll help you move it."

He lifted his end of the sofa in stunned silence. Once we had it in place, he asked with concern, "Are you OK? Do you have a headache?"

I chuckled, "I'm great, honey, never better. Can I get you a cup of coffee?"

Ron and I recently celebrated our 26th wedding anniversary, and I am happy to report that my "filter" is still in place—though it occasionally springs a leak. I've also expanded the filter principle beyond my marriage and found that it's especially useful when speaking to telemarketers, traffic cops, and teenagers.

● ● ●

Nancy learned a lesson Jeenie continually teaches in therapy: protecting the husband's ego. The egos of men and women are very different. Women's egos have emotional attachments to many women in their lives while men's egos are usually only emotionally connected to their wives.

In late boyhood, the male ego becomes encapsulated deep within—for protection. I liken the ego to a fragile egg. A man will allow his ego to emerge only at the onset of marriage when he is certain it will be safe with his wife.

Unfortunately, in marriage, a wife can begin to crush her husband's ego little by little, as Nancy did with her constant putdowns. In time, as her brother warned, her husband could refuse to continue in emotional abuse and leave the marriage for someone who will respect him.

As women, we do not completely understand this concept, but it is the crux of a good marriage. Even though a wife should be honest with her husband, in no way is it fair to attack his personhood.

IN THE NEXT STORY John and Karen found ways to build a stable marriage.

"I Love You More Today . . . "

Karen Kosman

As my husband, John, and I planned our 22nd wedding anniversary celebration, we praised God for His guidance throughout our marriage.

"John, remember how hard the first four months were?"

"How could I forget! Over the years we've shared the good and the bad. God has turned our weaknesses into strengths. We've matured together, Karen, in our faith and grown as individuals. And I love you more today than yesterday."

"I'm grateful God taught us to be flexible and transparent because we've been able to set an example that's influenced our friends and family."

John smiled, kissed me, and said, "I'm going to bed."

In the stillness of our living room my mind recalled those first four months of our marriage. Our wedding was a dream come true for both of us. After suffering from failed first marriages, we felt God had given us a second chance. We knew enough not to expect our lives to be perfect, but we certainly didn't expect to be miserable.

Within those first four months of our marriage, our past relationship struggles started popping up, which caused a lot of misunderstandings. It seemed we argued daily. The situation reached a crisis one Saturday while we were driving home from shopping. John had been talking about something, and I felt myself tune him out.

When John pulled into our driveway and turned off the car, he said, "Karen, I'm talking to you, and you haven't heard a word I've said."

"John, I'm sorry. I got distracted, but I did hear part of what you said. Please start over. You have my full attention now."

Frustrated, John got out of the car, and said, "I might as well wander off somewhere and disappear. You probably wouldn't even notice." Then he walked away angrily.

Liking the New Me

I sat there a moment, feeling hurt and angry myself. *I'm tired of constantly arguing.* "Lord, we need Your help," I prayed. Then I got out of the car and entered our apartment. I found John sitting on our bed. He looked up and said, "Karen, I asked God to show us why this is happening."

"I did, too. I realized that you and I react to stress differently. Often on weekends I tune out the world, even you, especially after pressure builds up at work all week."

"I know. I can speak for several minutes before I realize you're not listening. It makes me feel angry and abandoned. I'm sorry, Karen, for getting mad, but in certain situations, words or actions trigger bad memories."

"John, that's it. We keep replaying bad mental images from our past marriages. The old images hurt, and we lash out at each other." John sat there and nodded—and I knew he understood.

John and I had both grown up in alcoholic homes where verbal abuse caused feelings of abandonment. I'd learned to survive by tuning out during my parents' fights, and years later, by ignoring insults from my first husband. When John became angry, I'd retreated once again. It was a vicious cycle that kept repeating itself.

John's method of survival had been completely different than mine. He learned to stand firm and speak out.

Over time, we agreed not to stuff the old images down inside us but to discuss them with each other and pray about them. Instead of agreeing to disagree, we determined to uncover the problems and resolve them.

We wrote out a favorite Scripture verse and taped it to our bathroom mirror: *"But those who hope in the Lord will renew their strength. They will soar on wings like eagles; they will run and not grow weary, they will walk and not be faint"* (Isaiah 40:31).

We also sought Christian counseling, where we learned a communication game. The listener would describe the feelings and meaning of the speaker. If understood correctly, the speaker would say, "Bull's-eye." Then we'd reverse roles. It was fun, and it worked. Better communication led to another decision. We wrote a "marriage statement" to remind us of our first love in Christ and our commitment to each other:

- We recognize that Christ is the foundation of our marriage.
- We promise to pray for each other and study Scripture together daily.
- We agree to weekly meetings to discuss decisions, money matters, or anything that affects our future.
- We agree to confront any old images—and to erase them.
- We agree to take time out if a discussion becomes heated.
- We agree to sit down later, pray over the problem, and discuss it.
- We count our blessings—creating new memories along the way.

John and I understand how blessed we are to have overcome those obstacles that prevented us from communicating. Our victory is found in the faith, love, and hope we share in Christ. Those images are filled with new messages of joy. I'm blessed when I hear John say, "Karen, I love you more today than yesterday."

● ● ●

We all like to plan a trip, but we often can't foresee the inconveniences that may arise. Imagine the trip to Judah that Naomi and her daughters-in-law, Ruth and Orpah, took.

As the three women traveled along, Naomi silently pondered what had occurred in the ten years since her husband, Elimelech, moved his family to Moab. They had left Bethlehem to escape a famine, but soon after, Elimelech died. Recently her sons, Ruth's and Orpah's husbands, also had died.

Naomi was anxious to return to her home, but she struggled with the fairness of her decision to take Ruth and Orpah with her. How would she in her old age provide for them? She stopped suddenly and looked at her daughters-in-law with a new conviction. "Go back, each of you, to your mother's home. May the LORD show kindness to you, as you have shown to your dead and to me. May the LORD grant that each of you will find rest in the home of another husband" (Ruth 1:8–9).

Orpah tearfully decided to return to Moab, but Ruth refused and clung to her mother-in-law.

> But Ruth replied, "Don't urge me to leave you or to turn back from you. Where you go I will go, and where you stay I will stay. Your people will be my people and your God my God. . . . May the Lord deal with me, be it ever so severely, if anything but death separates you and me.
> —Ruth 1:16–17

Ruth's compassionate words were also words of conviction that have touched many hearts throughout history. Ruth understood that her husband would not be coming home. She would not see him again in her lifetime, but that did not sever family ties. It takes great confidence to leave everything you have known and go to a strange land with foreign people. Perhaps the years she'd spent with her husband had laid a foundation of trust in his God. "Your God will be my God," Ruth told Naomi.

Who can argue with a determined woman? So Ruth continued on with Naomi. As Naomi reached the outskirts of Bethlehem, familiar sights, sounds, and smells brought back memories, and she may have wondered, Will anyone recognize me?

But as the two women reached the town, excitement mounted and heads turned. Word spread, and the women of the town exclaimed, "Can this be Naomi?" (Ruth 1:19).

> "Don't call me Naomi, she told them. "Call me Mara, because the Almighty has made my life very bitter. I went

away full, but the LORD has brought me back empty. Why call me Naomi? The LORD has afflicted me; the Almighty has brought misfortune upon me."
—Ruth 1:20–21

The name Mara means "bitter," yet Naomi referred to God as the *Almighty*, showing reverence even in her deep sorrow.

When Boaz arrived to greet his harvesters, he noticed a young woman out in the fields following the harvesters. Boaz asked his foreman who the young woman was. The foreman said that Ruth was the Moabitess who came back with Naomi. Boaz walked over to Ruth and said:

"I've been told all about what you have done for your mother-in-law since the death of your husband—how you left your father and mother and your homeland and came to live with a people you did not know before. May the LORD repay you for what you have done. May you be richly rewarded by the LORD, the God of Israel, under whose wings you have come to take refuge."
—Ruth 2:11–12

Boaz instructed Ruth to glean only from his fields, and he provided food and water for her. He also gave orders to the harvesters that no one was to harm her.

When Ruth shared these events with Naomi, the elderly woman smiled, for she realized that Boaz might be the kinsman-redeemer who would marry Ruth. Naomi's prayers for God to provide Ruth a home and someone to care for her were about to be answered.

Eventually, Ruth married Boaz, and they had a son named Obed. When Naomi held her grandson in her arms, she no longer felt empty or bitter. From the bloodline of Ruth and Boaz came King David and eventually Jesus Christ.

Reflections

How has God given you new insight and helped you to like
who you are?

*I praise You, Lord, for giving me joy in
who I am.*

Wounded by Words

CHAPTER 12

Created in God's Image

My frame was not hidden from you
when I was made in the secret place.
   When I was woven together in the depths of the earth,
your eyes saw my unformed body.
   All the days ordained for me were written in your book
before one of them came to be.
                              —Psalm 139:15–16

A young mother-to-be leaves her doctor's office with a copy of the ultrasound image of her unborn baby. The obstetrician's words echo in her mind. "That's your baby's heart." What a special moment! She places her hand on her bulging waistline and smiles. Long before she'll hold her child or know the color of the eyes and hair, she's been introduced to the miracle of life, growing just below her own heart. Suddenly she feels a kicking sensation and knows that all is well.

God knew us before He formed us in our mother's womb. Isn't that an exciting thought? We read in Scripture that He knows the very number of hairs on our head. Science tells us as individuals we each have a unique set of fingerprints. Law enforcement uses those one-of-a-kind fingerprints for identification. Recently the design of the eye has been discovered to be uniquely different for each person too.

WITH THE KNOWLEDGE of these facts, we are given an inspiring glimpse of God's sovereignty. Though we can only attempt to plan for our children's futures, God has planned the best for our lives. However, He has given us free will, so we can alter His plans by making poor choices. Nevertheless, He promises to never leave or forsake us.

When we are going through difficult times, He is always by our side. He is the Potter, shaping and molding us, and good will result. His everlasting arms are wrapped tightly around us. We are His children who are created in His image.

> *It's in Christ that we find out who we are and what we are living for. Long before we first heard of Christ and got our hopes up, he had his eye on us, had designs on us for glorious living, part of the overall purpose he is working out in everything and everyone.*
> —Ephesians 1:11–12 (*The Message*)

LIFE AFTER DIVORCE is similar to pieces of broken pottery— except the shattered pieces are those of broken hearts, flattened by despair.

The Potter
Karen L. Kosman

The memory of my first husband's parting words haunted me: "I don't love you anymore, and maybe I never did."

Jeremiah 18:3–6 describes how God began healing me:

> *So I went down to the potter's house, and I saw him working at the wheel. But the pot he was shaping from the clay was marred in his hands; so the potter formed it into another pot, shaping it as seemed best to him.*
> —Jeremiah 18:3–6

God began sculpting away my marred self-image. He filled in the cracks that angry words had created.

My son Robert, daughter Linda, and I moved to Huntington Beach, where I found a new church. I'd hoped the change would bring renewal to my spirit. A few weeks later, a woman in my Sunday School class asked, "Don't you know that God hates divorce?"

I didn't want to go into all the years of pain that led to my divorce. "Yes," I replied, "and so do I."

She sat there looking like she had something else to say. Fortunately the class song leader stood, and we began singing.

Lord, help me to move forward. I don't want to feel angry toward a woman who has no understanding of me or my situation.

The following Sunday another woman approached me. I looked around for a route of escape, in case I needed to leave quickly. "Karen, I'm Irene, and I'd love to have you join our small singles group. We meet at the pastor's house on Tuesday evenings at 7:00.

I attended and became acquainted with two new friends, Randy and Jim. They understood my pain because they, too, had lived through the rejection of a spouse. We prayed together and talked about our children. In our small group, words were kind and encouraging.

As Christmas approached, I felt blessed to have this extended family. Yet I also felt sad because I worked long hours at a local hospital and didn't have enough time to spend with my kids.

My former husband, Ted, had joint custody, but never fulfilled his obligation to have his son and daughter every other weekend. Linda said, "I wouldn't go, anyway." Robert never expressed his feelings, but I saw the pain in his eyes.

This Christmas marked the second year since my divorce, and I'd hoped to buy a Christmas tree. Instead, I'd spent the money on presents.

After wrapping presents on Christmas Eve, I stood in the middle of our living room and thought, *I really miss having a tree.* Just then our front door opened, and in walked Robert, dragging a six-foot tree behind him.

"Mom, I worked at a tree lot today, and they paid me with this tree."

I knew that had not been an easy task for my 17-year-old son, who struggled with learning disabilities.

"Robert, what a wonderful surprise!"

Moments later Linda came out of the bedroom to see what was happening. Her face lit up. "A Christmas tree! Let's decorate it."

We busily put lights and ornaments on it while we listened to Christmas carols. I placed presents I'd wrapped for Robert and Linda under the tree. Irene stopped by with a $300 coupon book. She smiled and said, "Enjoy your Christmas."

Our apartment filled with the sweet smell of pine, and we laughed together.

After the kids went to bed, I sat in the living room with only the lights from the Christmas tree on. Reflections from the bulbs danced on the ceiling and walls. I reflected on one of God's promises: *"Never will I leave you; never will I forsake you"* (Hebrew 13:5).

After Christmas, Linda found a present addressed to her—one I'd forgotten to put under the tree. "Mom, I love my white nightshirt. It's my favorite present."

"Linda, really. Why is that?"

"It has *I love you* on the front."

I smiled because I realized the hands of the Master Potter were still reshaping our lives. Those special moments He'd brought into our lives over the past two years were part of His design—the message of love He engraved replaced the despair.

● ● ●

There are circumstances, such as Karen's divorce, over which we have no control. The good news is we have the choice as to how we will *respond* to the painful event. Karen learned the secret.

We've all heard the expression "from rags to riches." Demeaning words dress our spirits in rags, but God's love has the ability to make us rich in spirit. Andrea Chevalier shares how her dad's mean-spirited words caused her self-image to remain low until God began to heal her broken heart.

Walking Through the Pain
Andrea Chevalier

In high school, academically, I was always in the top 5 percent of my class. I sang in the elite choir and belonged to the drill team. Although, looking back, I realize these were good accomplishments, at the time, I felt like a failure because of my dad. He rarely complimented me; instead, he constantly made fun of me.

"You're getting too fat," he said one day in a nasty tone. Then he took me to the local school track and made me run until I could hardly walk, much less run, another step. Then on the way home, he reminded me of how I needed to start a diet.

A few days later he took me to a drugstore and had me take my blood pressure.

"Andrea, if you weren't so fat, your blood pressure wouldn't be so high."

In college I started attending a Bible study that talked about replacing all the negative thoughts in our heads with Scripture. Some friends in the group began to mentor me and helped me to see myself the way God intended me to be instead of the way my dad had portrayed me.

About three years later, I started teaching a Bible study at a maternity home for unwed mothers. I went with the intention of just teaching the young women and meeting a few new friends. However, God had other plans. As I listened to the women say things like, "I feel so worthless," and "I'll never accomplish my dreams," I realized they suffered as I once had.

My father's negative comments replayed in my mind. "Andrea, you'll never amount to anything, because you are worthless." Suddenly I understood that God wanted me to share with these women how He'd helped me become victorious over the verbal scars in my life.

I gave each woman a spiral notebook and explained, "Every time you have a negative thought, write it down in your journal. It may be caused by something a parent, friend, or boyfriend said to you, or it may just be a thought that popped into your mind. Either way, write it down. Then take your Bible and find a Scripture with a positive answer. Write the passage in your notebook and read it until God's image of you replaces the negative one."

For example, if they thought they were worthless, I told them to write down Psalm 139:1–3:

> O LORD, you have searched me
>   and you know me.
> You know when I sit and when I rise;
>   you perceive my thoughts from afar.
> You discern my going out and my lying down;
>   you are familiar with all my ways.
>   —Psalm 139:1–3

One of the women came back and told me, "I now carry my notebook in my purse everywhere I go. Whenever I am struggling, I make sure I have it with me so I can take it out and read through the Scripture passages."

Another woman wrote to me after she graduated from the program and said: "My journal is full. I have been able to write things down on paper that I have been feeling on the inside. It has helped me to release the pain and get past some of the things that I was holding onto. Now I am starting to see myself as God sees me."

Hearing comments like these has made me realize that God is capable of taking the hurt in our lives and transforming it to the good of others. By my willingness to let God use me to bring encouragement to these young women, I have overcome my past as God continues to heal my wounds.

● ● ●

Keeping a record is often Jeenie's recommendation to her clients in counseling. She says, "It brings us into reality and encourages us. It can be read numerous times and is life-changing. When God gives us advice through Scripture, we have a responsibility to write it down and allow it to saturate our lives."

MARTIN LUTHER SAID, "Peace, if possible, but the truth at any rate." In Audrey Ferguson's story we see the reality behind these powerful words.

Learning to Listen to the Truth
Audrey Ferguson

"You have the hugest legs in the world!"

For a few seconds, my world seemed to stop as I struggled to react to the words of my co-worker Carl. Unable to come up with a response, I simply looked at him.

I had only known Carl for about two weeks. Yet his words seemed to overshadow all the compliments that I had ever received. Before his comment, I had been focused on winning the volleyball game that I was playing with him and the rest of our college-aged co-workers. Within seconds, however, my priority became trying not to cry in front of everyone.

Perhaps it was the use of the word *huge* that made me feel devastated. Maybe it was because Carl had shared his opinion in front of 12 other people. Whatever the reason, Carl's words injured me in ways that no others had before. Only with God's amazing grace was I able to maintain my composure in front of both Carl and the others.

Later that evening, though, I cried myself to sleep. Upon waking the following morning, memories of the night before brought back the pain and feelings of rejection. Carl's crude statement, "You have the hugest legs in the world," lit a flame of doubt that Satan fueled with thoughts such as, *You are ugly, You are worthless,* and *No one could love you.* I began to see myself as "huge."

Everything within me fought against the idea of wearing shorts the next morning, even my modest shorts, because to do so would mean showing my legs. Upon discovering that I had no clean long pants, the condemning voices became louder.

However, as I pulled the shorts over my legs, one voice slowly began to dominate the others. *You are my child. Do not be ashamed of the shape I gave you. You are my beautiful child.* Even as I heard these words, they did not penetrate my heart immediately. That morning, I had to consciously choose to believe these words from God.

As I entered the cafeteria, I felt like everyone's eyes were on me, judging me as unacceptable. Each step toward the table became a deliberate step that required me to ask God for strength. Silently, I prayed, *Lord, do You promise that I am acceptable?*

Throughout those seconds that seemed like an eternity, He faithfully responded: *As My child, you are more than acceptable. You are loved.*

That morning choosing to eat became my second battle. Instead of food representing nourishment, it became the reason I wore size 12 jeans—obviously unacceptably large.

Lord, help me to view food and my body as something good.

He answered my prayers and affirmed me as His daughter.

When Carl called me huge, he broke my confidence, along with a part of my heart. Even as I am learning to see myself as God sees me, the memory of what Carl said still hurts. Yet, every time my heart stings with the memory of Carl's words, God faithfully reminds me that He sees me as His beautiful daughter. He is teaching me to listen to His truths.

* * *

How do we handle a negative comment? Jeenie says, "As soon as I find myself concentrating on a negative comment, I shut it out. Often I do something physical to get it out of my thoughts. Eventually, I think of it less and less, and it no longer has destructive power in my life."

"ONLY THOSE WHO have been the subject of constant name-calling and bullying can understand that each day is a dreaded event," states Dr. Debra Peppers. She experienced the pain of careless words, but also learned the power behind loving words.

The Power of a Word
Dr. Debra Peppers

"Fatso's back!"

"No, it's Jailbird now! Didn't you hear she spent the night in jail?"

Although I was used to such name-calling, my first day back at school after running away from home was especially difficult. As a confused, angry, and obese 16-year-old, my grades plummeted, and I gave up trying to overcome the taunts of my classmates. I became the bullies' target, eventually living up to the names I was called. To escape I began drinking, doing drugs, hanging out with the wrong crowd, and eventually running away from home.

My mom and dad were hardworking, middle-class parents who had been at school numerous times; had taken me to psychiatrists, doctors, and counselors; and had "bailed me out" of trouble or jail whenever they could. The last time I ran away I stayed hidden for six weeks. But with no money and nowhere to live, once again as the prodigal child, I found my way home. I agreed to follow their rules and reluctantly returned to school.

The first day back was as miserable as I had anticipated. Once again I heard the names and fat jokes as my peers jeered and laughed upon my return. I probably would have run away again had it not been for a familiar voice from the end of the hall.

Mrs. Alma Sitton—fondly called "Miss Alma"—was one teacher who had always treated me with respect and dignity. She was a great teacher and immersed us in literature, grammar, and speech. We all knew that if we missed one day of Miss Alma's class, she had the neat stacks of makeup work ready to distribute. Since I had been gone for weeks, I thought I would never catch up!

Ignoring the taunts of my classmates, I dutifully trudged down the hall as Miss Alma called to me. She ushered me into her warm, familiar classroom, near the table of missed assignments. I said nothing as I rolled my eyes, bit my tongue, and waited for a lecture. What came next was totally unexpected. Miss Alma turned toward me and did the most paradoxical, most unbelievable thing. She quietly closed the door, put her gentle hands on my shoulders, and looked in my eyes down to my soul. Then she hugged me! Softly in my ear she whispered, "Debbie, God has great plans for your life if you'll let Him, and I'm here for you, too. You are a talented, intelligent young woman, and you can succeed far beyond your own expectations." She assured me there would be no one disrespecting me in her classroom, and no matter what others said in the halls, I must remember how special I was to God.

I can't explain how this brief moment in time became a turning point in my life, but I now know that it prompted me to search my own soul. I began praying, attending church, and reading Scripture. I found what I had been seeking all my life—the peace that passes all understanding. I read about the power of the spoken word, and I vowed I would never be the one to speak shame or degradation toward anyone else as it had been spoken to me.

In the following years, everything about my life changed radically—from college, to marriage, to becoming a teacher myself. Upon my own retirement, I was one of only five teachers inducted into the National Teachers Hall of Fame. Who would ever have imagined that a 250-pound rebellious high school dropout with such negative nicknames would be named Teacher of the Year? It may have been a surprise to others that I of all people would become a high school teacher, but it was no surprise to Miss Alma.

After having lost 100 pounds, I was happily married and teaching in St. Louis, and I returned to my hometown to tell Miss Alma of this honor. I wanted her to know how those powerful words she had spoken to me had counteracted all the name-calling and negative words of my peers. I also shared that I led peer listening and mediation in my high school. And I thanked her for inspiring me to take a new road in life.

For the past ten years, I have also used the power of words as I host a daily call-in talk show in St. Louis and speak at women's conferences throughout the world. God has allowed me to share my story from Zimbabwe to El Salvador, from prisons to the Crystal Cathedral. I want everyone to know that no matter what negative words others have spoken of you, the word of God is what really matters. In turn, we are then able to use words in sharing God's love with other empty, hurting souls.

Two years ago was the biggest highlight of all. I was invited to speak at my high school reunion where Miss Alma was the guest of honor! I finally had the opportunity to tell my story and publicly thank her in front of the very ones who used to verbally attack me. Thanks to Miss Alma, I didn't want revenge. I wanted them to know that I forgave, just as I had been forgiven. As a teacher myself, I have now passed on the words of Miss Alma and the love of God to more than 10,000 other "Debbies."

Last October in El Salvador, I was privileged to speak to thousands where I told my story of Miss Alma. A young Hispanic girl came up to me with tears in her eyes and

said, "Did you know that the word *alma* means 'soul'?"
Somehow I was not surprised!

● ● ●

"Over the years I have practiced passing on compliments I hear regarding others," says Jeenie. "So often people will not give a direct tribute, but tell another person. So I let that person know the praise that was given them and by whom. It makes their day. Our words are indeed powerful."

Praise
Charles R. Brown

Let the words slowly escape
from your heart,
through your mind,
across your lips.

Praise be…
Praise be to the God…
Praise be to the Father…
Praise be to the God and Father
of our Lord Jesus Christ.
Listen carefully.
Hear those words:
Our Lord Jesus Christ.

God has blessed us in the heavens.
Look up with your heart,
through your soul.
You may find blessings
overlooked or forgotten.

God has blessed us—
blessed with *every* spiritual blessing
in Christ.
You are the beneficiary
of God's favor and goodness.
Praise!
You have been chosen in Him
before the world was made
to be holy—in Him
and blameless—through Him—
in His sight.

You are looked upon with
exceeding great favor.
In love, He planned before time
to adopt you, through Christ,
because He wanted to.
Praise His glorious grace.

Praise!
Grace has been given freely.
Praise be to God!

UNDERSTANDING IS A GIFT that God granted Susan—one that helped her overcome her mother's verbal attacks.

Gaining Understanding
Susan Titus Osborn

Mother looked at me and frowned. "Why do you look so much like your father? All your mannerisms remind me of him."

That question really had no answer, and I momentarily regretted inviting my mother to visit me in California. I didn't have any control over how I looked. My dad had died in an accident in 1964. Thirty years later, I had wonderful memories of a very special man, not his little mannerisms. But I had a feeling these issues went deeper than Mother's surface comments. I began to understand why my mother behaved the way she did.

In 1962, my parents divorced. In 1963 Daddy's business partner died and so did his oil business. Overnight, Mother went from being well off to struggling financially. Mother blamed all her problems on my dad.

The following year, Daddy took a new job in Arizona. One night he called Mother, asking if they could get back together. She said, "I never want to hear from you again. I hope you drop dead."

And the next day, he did. While hiking in the mountains and taking pictures to send to my sister and me, Daddy stood on a ledge that gave way. He fell 200 feet to his death. At the time I felt devastated at losing my dad—my best friend. I didn't take my mother's feelings into consideration at all.

But looking back, I tried to see her viewpoint. *She must have terrible guilt feelings about Daddy*, I thought, *and since I look so much like him, she is reminded of him every time she looks at me. Plus, my faith in God has brought me contentment— something her money could never buy.*

The next day I took Mother to the airport. She returned home feeling as miserable as when she arrived. Yet, I had a better understanding of her. Her verbal abuse wasn't directed at who I am so much as what I represented. She looked at me and saw my dad. She looked at my happiness and saw her own unhappiness.

I couldn't solve her problems, nor could I stop her from drinking. But I could show empathy toward her, and I could pray for her—every night. And I did for the rest of her life.

After my divorce, a psychologist helped me make a shocking discovery. I had married my mother! For the first 20 years of my life, I had lived with verbal abuse from my mother. The next 20 years, my husband dished out the same verbal abuse. At first I didn't recognize that truth because it was all I had ever known. But once I removed myself from the situation, with the help of a Christian psychologist I realized to my horror how my first husband's verbal abuse and treatment of me mirrored that of my mother.

After being single for 6 years, I am blessed with a wonderful, godly husband, who I've been married to for 15 years. I thank God every day for bringing Dick into my life. He is supportive of my writing and even edits my work. I never would have thought to ask God to bring me someone who reads the Bible with a Greek lexicon and does crossword puzzles in ink. But that's exactly what God did.

Dick suffered verbal abuse in his background, and when we are reminded of an incident from one of our pasts, we discuss it, pray about it, and work through it. I don't believe you ever forget the past, but once you have removed yourself from the situation and forgiven those who wronged you, with God's help, you can begin to heal.

Today, I am healed, and I sense that God is calling me to nurture and encourage others who are walking where I once walked. Because I understand their pain, with God's guidance, perhaps I can pass that help onto them.

● ● ●

Possessed is defined in the *Random House Dictionary* as "spurred or moved by a strong feeling, madness, or a supernatural power." In the New Testament, Mary Magdalene is described as a woman possessed by seven demons—

not exactly the qualifications to win a popularity contest. In other biblical accounts mentioning demons, we read of torment and isolation. We can assume that a woman under these circumstances would be feared and even ridiculed. Who could accept and help her? Who could wipe away her tears and set her free of her tormentors?

Mary Magdalene, a woman of means, knew the pain of being possessed. Seven demons fought within her mind, body, and soul. We can only imagine that internally her emotions became twisted. She must have ached constantly because of the lack of understanding, her heart burning with a desire for someone to set her free.

Scripture is silent on how Mary met Jesus or the circumstances surrounding her healing. Perhaps she met Him in a throng of people who crowded together to see, hear, and be touched by Jesus. Whatever the circumstances, Mary personally met Jesus—a moment that transformed her life forever. His compassionate, healing touch and His powerful words set her free.

What happened to Mary after her extraordinary encounter with Jesus?

> *After this, Jesus traveled about from one town and village to another, proclaiming the good news of the kingdom of God. The Twelve were with him, and also some women who had been cured of evil spirits and diseases: Mary (called Magdalene) from whom seven demons had come out; Joanna the wife of Cuza, the manager of Herod's household; Susanna; and many others. These women were helping to support them out of their own means.*
> —Luke 8:1–3

Mary became a woman of faith—her strength renewed and her hope fulfilled. Her love transformed her into a woman of action, and later brought her to the foot of the cross.

"Near the cross of Jesus stood his mother, his mother's sister, Mary the wife of Clopas, and Mary Magdalene" (John 19:25).

They stood there at the Cross, watching with anguish, feeling helpless and asking the question, "Why?" They heard His words, *"It is finished."* Day turned to night. The earth itself shook under their trembling bodies.

Then early on the first day of the week, before the sun rose, Mary Magdalene was among some women who carried spices to anoint the body of Jesus. When they approached the tomb, they found it empty. Surprise and shock engulfed them with fear. Surreal events unfolded—rapid heartbeats, running feet, the disciples' questions, and disbelief—all within a short span of time. Then stillness, as Mary stood alone by the tomb wondering, *Where have they taken my Lord?* Desperately trying to hold onto hope, her tears fell. Slight movement. *Someone is standing there in the garden, but who is he?*

> *"Woman,"* he said, *"why are you crying? Who is it you are looking for?"*
>
> *Thinking he was the gardener, she said, "Sir, if you have carried him away, tell me where you have put him, and I will get him."*
>
> *Jesus said to her, "Mary."*
>
> *She turned toward him and cried out in Aramaic, "Rabboni!" (which means Teacher).*
> —John 20:15–16

When Jesus said her name, Mary immediately recognized Him.

What does Mary Magdalene's story have to do with verbal abuse?

- At one time Mary had no hope.
- Her problems had seemed insurmountable.
- Christ set her free.

For those who suffer from emotional abuse, their spirits are crushed—their problems, too, seem insurmountable. The negative results of verbal cruelty and emotional abuse entangle the lives of the abused with rejection, false accusations, fear, anger, demeaning words, manipulation, and lack of confidence. These are some of the demons of emotional exploitation.

We need to become women of action and courage. Hope is a phone call away, while courage is rekindled in a therapist's office. A counselor once told Karen, "Tears are the raindrops of angels." Finding our boldness in speaking out is God giving us wings.

The good news is we do not need to suffer in silence, and we do not need to travel the road of recovery alone. Close your eyes and listen. Jesus is calling your name.

Reflections

How has God helped you to see yourself as He sees you?

*Thank You, Lord, for teaching me that
I am Your child—created in Your image.*

New Hope® Publishers is a division of WMU®,
an international organization that challenges Christian believers
to understand and be radically involved in God's mission.
For more information about WMU, go to www.wmu.com.
More information about New Hope books may be found
at www.newhopepublishers.com. New Hope books
may be purchased at your local bookstore.

BOOKS TO
{ Heal You }

Refuge
*A Pathway Out of Domestic
Violence and Abuse*
Detective Sergeant Donald Stewart
ISBN-10: 1-56309-811-3
ISBN-13: 978-1-56309-811-3

**A Woman with a Past,
A God with a Future**
Embracing God's Transforming Love
Elsa Kok
ISBN-10: 1-59669-001-1
ISBN-13: 978-1-59669-001-1

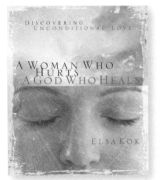

**A Woman Who Hurts,
A God Who Heals**
Discovering Unconditional Love
Elsa Kok
ISBN-10: 1-56309-950-0
ISBN-13: 978-1-56309-950-2

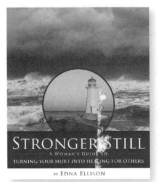

Stronger Still
*A Woman's Guide to Turning Your
Hurt into Healing for Others*
Edna Ellison
ISBN-10: 1-59669-090-9
ISBN-13: 978-1-59669-090-5

Available in bookstores everywhere
For information about these books or any New Hope®
product, visit www.newhopepublishers.com.